COOL BRITANNIA AND BEYOND

BRITAIN IN THE 1990S

S A CARMODY

KMCS PUBLISHING

First published in Great Britain in 2025 by

KMCS Publishing

ISBN: 978-1-0681917-7-0 Paperback

ISBN: 978-1-0681917-8-7 eBook

Printed and bound in the United Kingdom

The moral right of the author has been asserted.

INTRODUCTION – WELCOME TO THE NINETIES

The 1990s were the last analogue decade and the first digital one. They began with Margaret Thatcher's tearful departure from Downing Street in 1990 and ended with Tony Blair's triumphant stride into the new millennium. In between, Britain was remade politically, economically, socially, culturally, technologically. It was a decade of contradictions, optimism, anxiety, swagger, and sorrow, hope, and backlash. A decade that bridged the world of corner shops and VHS tapes with one of mobiles, modems, and globalisation.

This book tells the story of that transformation.

A Decade of Change

The 90s reshaped almost every aspect of British life. In politics, John Major's "grey man" premiership was rocked by sleaze, Europe, and Black Wednesday, while Tony Blair's "New Labour" perfected spin and swept to power in a landslide. The Good Friday Agreement promised peace in Northern Ireland, even as bombs still tore through cities.

The economy lurched from early-90s recession to late-90s boom. The pound crashed, unemployment soared, and

BSE destroyed trust in food. But by decade's end, Britain was a nation of Starbucks coffee, IKEA wardrobes, Sunday shopping, and optimism that "Cool Britannia" could compete with anyone.

Culture was louder and brasher than ever. Britpop turned Blur and Oasis into household names, the Spice Girls sold Girl Power to the world, and Tracey Emin's My Bed made headlines as art. TV shows from Friends to The Royle Family shaped how we spoke and laughed, while tabloids and paparazzi redefined fame. Celebrity was everywhere and nowhere more so than in the story of Princess Diana, who harnessed the media to her cause and then fell victim to it.

Technology crept from offices into homes, and then into pockets. PCs and Windows 95 made computing mainstream, mobiles went from bricks to everyday tools, and the internet slowly spread from universities to suburban bedrooms. The PlayStation created a new generation of gamers, Napster shook the music industry, and Dolly the Sheep proved cloning wasn't science fiction anymore.

Sport became spectacle. Italia '90 gave us Gazza's tears, Euro '96 gave us "football's coming home," and Manchester United's Treble gave us drama that felt scripted. Women's sport made quiet but crucial breakthroughs: England's women won the Rugby World Cup in 1994, and their cricketers triumphed in 1993, even if they barely made the back pages.

Tragedy marked the decade too. The Dunblane massacre led to sweeping gun reforms. The murder of Stephen Lawrence forced the country to confront institutional racism. The James Bulger case left the nation horrified at what children could do. IRA bombs struck Warrington, Manchester, and Omagh. And Diana's death in 1997 provoked unprecedented grief and a reckoning with the monarchy itself.

Women and Voices of Change

Women's experiences are woven through every part of the 1990s story. Mo Mowlam played a central role in the Northern Ireland peace process. "Blair's Babes" doubled women's representation in Parliament. Female athletes provided new role models on television, even as coverage remained patchy. Diana challenged the stigma around HIV/AIDS and landmines, while activists fought Section 28 and campaigned for LGBTQ+ rights.

At the same time, the media sexualised, trivialised, and scrutinised women relentlessly, from lad mags' pin-ups to ladettes' drinking habits. Women entered the workforce in record numbers, but often on insecure contracts, juggling childcare with jobs in retail and services. Their progress was real, but incomplete; visible but contested.

Why the 90s Still Matter

The 1990s didn't just entertain; they created the framework we still live in today. Black Wednesday's humiliation and Maastricht's divisions fed directly into Brexit. The spin machine of New Labour became the Twitter (X) and TikTok politics of the 2020s. Flexible work arrangements became today's gig economy. Celebrity magazines became Instagram. Diana's public mourning foreshadowed social media grief.

Every time England fans sing "football's coming home," every time a supermarket shelves global food, every time a smartphone pings with a text, every time politics feels like performance we are living with the legacy of the 1990s.

How This Book Works

Each chapter tells part of this story: politics and power, economy and everyday life, culture and identity, science and health, sport and spectacle, tragedy and shock. The focus is Britain, but global events such as the end of the Cold War,

Rwanda, Kosovo, Hong Kong's handover are never far from view.

At the end of each chapter is a mini-timeline: a snapshot of key dates and moments. Read them as a quick reference, memory prompts, or parallel narratives of the decade. Together, they form a mosaic of the 1990s, not exhaustive, but representative, capturing the shocks, breakthroughs, and turning points that made the decade unforgettable.

The Spirit of the Nineties

The 1990s were messy, noisy, contradictory, and transformative. They didn't solve Britain's problems, but they made change visible and possible. They taught the country to live with uncertainty, diversity, and digital disruption.

This book doesn't aim to tidy the decade into a simple story because the 90s weren't simple. Instead, it explores the tensions and legacies of a decade when Britain stepped into modernity, not smoothly, but stumbling, laughing, crying, and reinventing itself along the way.

Welcome back to the nineties.

1. POLITICS AND POWER

*T*he 1990s were a turning point in British politics. They began with the fall of Margaret Thatcher, the most dominant figure of the post-war era, and ended with the rise of Tony Blair, a Prime Minister who seemed less a politician than a media phenomenon. In between came riots, economic shocks, sleaze scandals, constitutional upheavals, and the fragile hope of peace in Northern Ireland. If the 1980s had been about ideology, the 1990s became about image and Britain has never looked back.

THE FALL of the Iron Lady (1990)

Margaret Thatcher's resignation in November 1990 marked the end of an era. After eleven years in power, she was forced out not by the electorate but by her own Conservative Party, exhausted by her authoritarian style and deep divisions over Europe.

Her downfall was hastened by the Community Charge, better known as the Poll Tax. Designed as a flat-rate local tax, it meant a duke paid the same as a dustman, and resentment boiled over. On 31 March 1990, between 70,000 and 200,000 protesters marched on the streets of London. The demonstration, intended to be peaceful, descended into the Poll Tax riots when clashes broke out in Trafalgar Square. Police vans were overturned, shops looted, and riot officers charged through smoke-filled streets. It was one of the largest and most violent demonstrations in late-20th-century London, a visible sign that Thatcher's authority was broken.

Her successor, John Major, presented himself as the anti-Thatcher: quieter, consensual, even a little dull. But Britain was ready for boring after the battles of the 1980s.

JOHN MAJOR: Grey Man in a Noisy Decade

Major, the boy from Brixton who had left school at sixteen, brought a gentler tone to government. Yet his premiership was haunted by crises.

In 1992, he won an unexpected election victory, but months later came humiliation on Black Wednesday. Britain crashed out of the European Exchange Rate Mechanism, the pound collapsed, and billions were spent in vain trying to defend it. Speculators like George Soros made fortunes betting against sterling. For a party that prided itself on economic competence, the disaster was devastating.

Major also faced the collapse of his "Back to Basics" campaign in 1993. Launched as a call for traditional values, it quickly became a punchline as Conservative MPs were caught in scandals involving sex, money, and corruption. Sleaze became the defining word of his government.

And yet, Major achieved more than his critics admitted. Against the odds, he nudged forward the Northern Ireland peace process, laying groundwork that Blair would later convert into the Good Friday Agreement. History has been kinder to Major than his contemporaries ever were.

THE SPIN MACHINE (1994–97)

By the mid-1990s, the Conservatives looked tired, divided, and toxic. Into the vacuum stepped Tony Blair, who became Labour leader in 1994 after the sudden death of John Smith. Blair rebranded his party as New Labour: pro-business, tough on crime, socially liberal, and media-savvy to a fault.

For Blair, politics was performance. Telegenic, articulate, and perfectly tuned to the rhythms of a 24-hour news cycle, he cut a figure unlike any British leader before him. With Alastair Campbell orchestrating communications, every photo op, soundbite, and headline was part of a strategy. For the first time, politics looked less like the House of Commons and more like prime-time television: a contest of presentation as much as policy.

In May 1997, Labour swept to power in a landslide, winning 418 seats, its biggest majority in history. The Conservatives were reduced to their lowest seat total since 1906 with just 165. Blair strode into Downing Street declaring, "A new dawn has broken, has it not?" Cool Britannia was in full swing, and Blair rode its wave, inviting Oasis to Downing Street and posing as the face of a modern Britain. To many, he represented optimism after the grey drizzle of Major's years. To others, he already seemed a little too slick.

ALL-WOMEN SHORTLISTS (1997)

It was also a new dawn for women in Parliament. Labour's bold experiment with all-women shortlists, introduced in the early 1990s to tackle chronic under-representation, transformed the Commons in 1997. Thanks to the policy, 101 female Labour MPs were elected, doubling the total number of women in Parliament overnight to 120. The tabloids patronisingly dubbed them "Blair's Babes," but the symbolism was profound: for the first time, women were not political tokens but a visible force. Issues like childcare, domestic violence, and workplace rights gained mainstream prominence.

The policy had not been without controversy. In 1996, it was challenged in the case of Jepson v The Labour Party, when two men excluded from selection argued that the scheme breached the Sex Discrimination Act 1975. The Industrial Tribunal agreed, ruling that under existing law shortlists could not legally exclude men. As a result, the policy was suspended.

Yet many of the women already selected under the scheme went on to stand in 1997, reshaping Parliament in the process. The Sex Discrimination (Election Candidates) Act 2002, which exempted political candidate selection from the 1975 law, later restored the principle. The controversy highlighted both the urgency of change and the legal obstacles to achieving it.

The Good Friday Agreement (1998)

Blair's greatest achievement of the decade was in Northern Ireland. The Good Friday Agreement, signed on 10 April 1998, was the culmination of years of delicate negotiations involving London, Dublin, Washington, and the province's rival parties. It ended three decades of conflict that had killed over 3,500 people. Power-sharing, decommissioning of weapons and prisoner releases. None of it was easy, but for the first time peace seemed within reach.

The settlement was endorsed by the people as well as

politicians. On May 22, 1998, simultaneous referendums were held. In Northern Ireland, turnout was an extraordinary 81%, with 71.1% voting Yes to the deal; in the Republic of Ireland, turnout was 55.6%, with 94.4% voting Yes to amend the constitution and remove territorial claims over the North. It was a moment of rare democratic clarity: north and south of the border, voters backed compromise and a shared future.

The Agreement also highlighted the role of women in politics. Mo Mowlam, the Secretary of State for Northern Ireland, became a household name for her plain speaking and courage. She visited prisoners in the Maze, brought warring factions into the same room, and won respect across divides. The Northern Ireland Women's Coalition, a cross-community party formed only two years earlier, secured seats at the negotiating table and pushed issues like victims' rights and integrated education. Though often overshadowed in the official narrative, many contemporaries credited these women with being the human bridge that made peace possible.

HOUSE OF LORDS REFORM (1999)

Blair's government also pushed through a constitutional change that, while less glamorous than Cool Britannia, was deeply significant: the reform of the House of Lords. For centuries, aristocrats had inherited their seats, turning the upper chamber into a bastion of hereditary privilege. In 1999, most of those peers were swept away. The Lords remained unelected, but suddenly it was less about dukes and earls and more about appointed life peers, many of them women and people from outside the establishment. It was a symbolic step towards modernisation and unfinished business that marked the end of an era.

.   .   .

Why It Mattered

The politics of the 1990s left deep marks. Thatcher's fall showed the limits of ideology. Major's struggles exposed the fragility of authority in an age of rolling news and scandal. Blair's rise demonstrated the power of image and spin, lessons every politician since has absorbed.

The Good Friday Agreement showed that even the bloodiest conflicts can move towards peace though Brexit has since put that fragile balance under pressure. And the obsession with "presentation" born in the Blair years still defines British politics today, where a viral clip or headline can end a career faster than a policy failure.

Mini Timeline – Politics and Power

1990 – Margaret Thatcher resigns; John Major becomes Prime Minister.

1990 – Poll Tax riots erupt in Trafalgar Square.

1992 – Conservatives win General Election, Black Wednesday pounds sterling.

1993 – Major's "Back to Basics" campaign backfires amid scandals.

1994 – Tony Blair becomes Labour leader.

1997 – Labour landslide; 101 female Labour MPs elected via all-women shortlists.

1998 – Good Friday Agreement signed and endorsed by referendum.

1999 – House of Lords hereditary peers removed.

2. ECONOMY: BOOM, BUST, AND RECOVERY

*he early 1990s hit Britain hard. Businesses folded, unemployment soared, and Black Wednesday humiliated the pound. Yet out of the wreckage came resilience. Britain's economy retooled around finance, services, and shopping. By the late 1990s, with Blair talking up Cool Britannia, prosperity boomed. But the new prosperity came with scars: regional divides, insecure jobs, and a widening gap between London and everywhere else.

RECESSION AND REDUNDANCY (1990–92)

The decade began with Britain slipping into its deepest slump since the early 1980s and was described, at the time, as the second worst recession since World War II. The boom of the late 1980s, fuelled by Chancellor Nigel Lawson's tax cuts and cheap credit, ended in a housing crash. Families found themselves in negative equity, trapped with mortgages bigger than the value of their homes.

Unemployment surged, peaking above three million by 1992. Factories closed, small businesses went under, and communities already scarred by the 1980s downturn sank further into hardship. High interest rates, meant to control inflation and keep sterling tied to the European Exchange Rate Mechanism, squeezed households mercilessly.

For women, the impact was mixed. Men in manufacturing and heavy industry were often the first to lose jobs, but women in part-time retail and service roles were also vulnerable, especially as local councils slashed budgets and public sector cuts hit care work, nursing, and teaching. Women were increasingly the ones holding families together on part-time wages, juggling insecure work with childcare. This pattern of flexibility at the cost of security would define much of the 1990s labour market.

Black Wednesday and the Pound's Fall (1992)

On 16 September 1992, forever known as Black Wednesday, Britain was forced out of the Exchange Rate Mechanism (ERM). The government raised interest rates from 10% to 12% in the morning, then to an eye-watering 15% in the afternoon, but currency traders remained unconvinced. After a £22 billion intervention, Chancellor Norman Lamont announced at 7:40 pm that Britain would leave the ERM.

Speculators like George Soros (an American-Hungarian investor who later became known as The Man Who Broke the Bank of England) made fortunes betting against sterling, with Soros pocketing over £1 billion. The Treasury's eventual estimate of losses was £3.3 billion and was a humiliation for a party that prided itself on economic competence.

Paradoxically, the collapse also paved the way for recovery. Freed from the ERM, interest rates could fall, exports became more competitive, and growth slowly returned. Lamont later claimed he was "singing in the bath" after the crisis, as the economy began to pick up. But the political damage was permanent. The Conservatives never regained their reputation for fiscal credibility, and Labour held consistent poll leads for the rest of the decade.

More importantly, Black Wednesday taught a lasting lesson: global financial markets could punish governments overnight. The vulnerability felt in 1992 would echo again during later crises, from the 2008 financial crash to the market turmoil of Brexit.

Mad Cow Disease and Economic Panic (1996)

The fragility of recovery was exposed again in 1996, when Britain was struck by the BSE crisis, or "mad cow disease." When scientists confirmed that BSE could be passed to humans in the form of variant CJD, panic set in. Beef exports were banned across Europe, supermarkets stripped shelves, and farming communities faced devastation.

The government's reassurances that British beef was safe rang hollow after years of denial. The crisis was not only a public health disaster but also an economic earthquake for agriculture. Entire livelihoods vanished, and rural Britain bore the brunt. For consumers, BSE shattered trust in food and official statements, fuelling later resistance to GM crops and other innovations.

From Industry to Services

Through the 1990s, Britain's economy shifted decisively away from manufacturing and towards finance, services, and consumption. London boomed as a global financial capital, its skyline reshaped by new towers and its workforce filled with young professionals. But while the City thrived, many regional towns, scarred by the factory closures of the 1980s, struggled to keep up.

Retail became a major engine of growth. Out-of-town shopping centres like the Trafford Centre (opened 1998) and was Europe's largest at the time. It symbolised a new age of consumerism. The Sunday Trading Act 1994 allowed shops to open on Sundays, cementing shopping as a leisure activity as much as a necessity.

Women, already dominant in retail employment, found new opportunities but these were often in low-paid, insecure positions. The feminisation of the workforce was one of the quiet revolutions of the 1990s economy, but it came without equal pay or job security. Glass ceilings remained firmly in place.

The Blair–Brown Revolution (1997–99)

When Labour swept to power in 1997, they inherited a growing economy. Chancellor Gordon Brown made two immediate decisions that reshaped the landscape: he gave the Bank of England independence to set interest rates (May 1997), and he committed to sticking with Conservative spending limits for his first two years. These moves reassured nervous markets and sceptical voters that Labour could be trusted with money.

But Brown was also quietly transformative. He channelled new investment into schools, hospitals, and family support. The National Minimum Wage (April 1999, £3.60 per hour for adults) lifted millions out of poverty pay, particularly women concentrated in part-time or service jobs. Working Families Tax Credit and childcare support eased pressure on households. His "golden rule" of borrowing only to invest over the economic cycle, provided a balance of discipline and ambition.

Women in politics drove much of this agenda. Harriet Harman championed childcare and workplace equality.

Female Labour MPs brought issues long dismissed as "domestic" into mainstream economic debate. The change wasn't revolutionary, but it was significant: for the first time, government recognised that the economy was not just about the City, but about family budgets and women's working lives.

The Cost of Prosperity

By the late 1990s, Britain looked richer. Starbucks and Gap spread across high streets, EasyJet (founded 1995) opened Europe to weekend breaks, and credit cards became household essentials. Cool Britannia wasn't just about music and fashion; it was about the confidence to spend, travel, and consume.

The National Lottery, launched in 1994, added another layer of aspiration. Millions tuned in each week, chasing millionaire dreams, while billions of pounds flowed into arts, sport, and community projects. The Lottery was criticised as a "tax on the poor," but it reshaped Britain's cultural and sporting infrastructure, laying the groundwork for Olympic success a decade later.

Yet prosperity was uneven. London and the South East surged ahead, while deindustrialised towns in the North, Scotland, and Wales lagged behind. The rise of zero-hour contracts, agency work, and temping brought flexibility but also insecurity. Women were overrepresented in these jobs, carrying the double burden of unstable wages and ongoing childcare responsibilities.

Female workforce participation reached 68% by 1997, but the gender pay gap persisted at around 17% for full-time workers. Finance and senior business roles remained dominated by men. Even as women entered the workforce in record numbers, the levers of economic power continued to be overpoweringly male.

The Millennium Bug: Economic Anxiety (1999)

As the decade closed, the economy faced a threat that wasn't a crash or a scandal, but a computer glitch. The Millennium Bug, the fear that computers would fail when the date rolled from "99" to "00" prompted businesses and government to spend billions reprogramming systems. Airlines, banks, hospitals, and utilities prepared for chaos.

When midnight struck on January 1, 2000, little went wrong. But the scare revealed how dependent Britain had become on technology. The Bug, that wasn't a bug, highlighted both the vulnerabilities and the new realities of a digital economy.

Why It Mattered

The economy of the 1990s was a story of survival, reinvention, and division. The early recession and Black Wednesday undermined faith in the Conservatives, paving the way for New Labour. The shift to a service-driven economy created jobs but left entire regions behind.

For women, the decade was paradoxical. They entered the workforce in record numbers, and policies like the minimum wage and childcare support improved their lives. Yet many remained concentrated in insecure and low-paid jobs.

The scars of the 1990s, regional inequality, insecure work, reliance on consumer spending still shape Britain today. The recovery was real, but uneven. The decade built a flexible, service-driven economy that promised opportunity but often delivered insecurity.

. . .

MINI TIMELINE – Economy

1990–92 – Deep recession; unemployment passes 3 million.

1992 – Black Wednesday (16 September); pound forced out of ERM, £3.3bn loss.

1993 – John Major launches "Back to Basics" campaign.

1994 – Sunday Trading Act allows Sunday shopping; National Lottery launches.

1996 – BSE crisis devastates farming.

1997 – Labour landslide; Gordon Brown gives Bank of England independence (May).

1999 – National Minimum Wage introduced (April) at £3.60/hour, Millennium Bug panic.

3. MUSIC AND CULTURE: THE BRITPOP YEARS

⁓

*I*f the 1980s had been all about synth-pop, yuppies and neon, the 1990s swaggered onto the stage with guitars, bucket hats, and a Union Jack minidress. This was the decade when British culture rediscovered its confidence, exporting music, film, and fashion to the world. Britpop, Girl Power, and gritty realism in cinema gave Britain a new identity. "Cool Britannia." But beneath the swagger lay contradictions: laddishness clashed with feminism, mainstream success with underground rebellion, and hype with reality.

POWER BALLADS AND CHART GIANTS: **The Early 90s**

The decade began with a softer anthem that refused to leave the charts. Bryan Adams' "(Everything I Do) I Do It for You" from the Robin Hood: Prince of Thieves soundtrack. It was released in July 1991 and went on to spend 16 consecutive weeks at No.1 in the UK, a record still unbeaten.

The early-90s period was dominated by international superstars. Whitney Houston's I Will Always Love

You (1992) became one of the biggest singles of all time, Madonna reinvented herself with Erotica (1992) and Ray of Light (1998), Michael Jackson's Dangerous (1991) tour filled stadiums, and grunge bands like Nirvana momentarily rewrote the rules of global rock. Britain listened, bought, and danced, but its own voice felt missing from the soundtrack.

BRITPOP: Oasis, Blur, and Beyond

By the mid-1990s, British music answered back. The rise of Britpop was, in part, a reaction to American dominance: Nirvana's angst, Pearl Jam's grunge, and Garth Brooks' country ballads ruled the airwaves. Blur, Oasis, Pulp, and Suede reclaimed the charts with a swaggering Englishness that stood in contrast to imported sounds. Suddenly, British accents, British references, and British humour mattered again.

The mid-1990s rise of Britpop remains a distinctly British sound that mixed jangly guitars, cheeky humour, and swaggering confidence. Blur's Parklife (1994) celebrated Englishness in all its eccentricity, while Oasis roared out of Manchester with working-class anthems like Wonderwall and Don't Look Back in Anger.

The Oasis vs. Blur "Battle of Britpop" in August 1995 wasn't just a chart rivalry; it became a cultural referendum: North vs. South, working-class vs. art school, lager vs. latte. Blur's Country House outsold Oasis's Roll with It by 58,000 copies, but Oasis ultimately achieved greater commercial success. The tabloids played it up, and suddenly music was front-page news. Oasis's concerts at Knebworth in August 1996 drew 250,000 fans over two nights, with 2.5 million people applying for tickets.

Yet Britpop was never just about men with guitars. Elastica, led by Justine Frischmann, scored a number one debut album. Sleeper, with Louise Wener at the helm, challenged the lad culture around them, insisting women weren't just muses but voices in their own right. Still, much of the scene was drenched in male bravado, and women artists often fought twice as hard for recognition.

Spice Mania and Girl Power

If Britpop swaggered, the Spice Girls screamed. Bursting onto the scene in 1996 with Wannabe, they became a global phenomenon overnight, eventually becoming the best-selling girl group in history with over 100 million records sold worldwide. "Girl Power" was their mantra, a mix of pop feminism, cheeky fun, and unapologetic ambition.

For millions of young girls, the Spice Girls offered something new: role models who were loud, funny, independent, and confident. Each Spice had an identity, Sporty, Scary, Baby, Posh, Ginger, and together they made individuality fashionable. In a decade dominated by "lad culture" and men's magazines, the Spice Girls turned the spotlight back to women's voices and buying power.

Their impact stretched beyond music. They reshaped marketing (Pepsi campaigns, merchandise everywhere), influenced fashion (platform trainers, Union Jack dress), and even politics. Tony Blair's Labour courted the Spice Girls as part of its "Cool Britannia" branding, proof that pop culture and politics were now inseparable.

The Rise of Club Culture

While Britpop and Girl Power dominated the charts, another scene was thriving underground: dance music and rave culture. Warehouse parties, Ibiza trips, and superclubs like Cream in Liverpool and Ministry of Sound in London defined nights out. The Criminal Justice Act 1994 attempted to crack down on illegal raves, but club culture continued to flourish in legal venues.

Women DJs and producers were still rare, but women were central to the club scene as dancers, promoters, and fans. The rave ethos of inclusivity, all genders, races, and classes under one strobe light, was a quiet rebellion against mainstream laddishness. Yet media coverage often reduced female ravers to fashion shots rather than recognising their creative roles.

CINEMA: From Trainspotting to The Full Monty

British film enjoyed a renaissance in the 1990s, supported by National Lottery funding from 1995. Trainspotting (1996), with its raw depiction of heroin addiction, shocked and thrilled audiences. The Full Monty (1997) turned unemployed Sheffield steelworkers into unlikely strippers and box office gold, earning over $250 million worldwide. Four Weddings and a Funeral (1994) made Hugh Grant the king of rom-coms and became the highest-grossing British film at that time. Shakespeare in Love (1998, an American-British co-production) won Best Picture at the Oscars.

Women were part of this revival, but often still behind the scenes. Screenwriters like Debbie Horsfield and directors like Antonia Bird (Priest, Face) broke ground. On screen, actresses like Emma Thompson (winning Oscars for Sense and Sensibility) and Kate Winslet (from Heavenly Creatures to Titanic) brought complex female roles into the spotlight. Yet the male-centred "lad" narrative still dominated, whether in football terraces or drug dens.

MAGAZINES, Media, and Lad Culture

The mid-90s saw the rise of lad culture, cheeky, blokey, irreverent. Magazines like Loaded (launched 1994) and FHM sold millions with covers featuring scantily clad women alongside beer jokes and football banter. Loaded's circulation peaked at 463,000 in 1998, while FHM reached over 750,000. The tone spilled over into comedy (Men Behaving Badly), advertising, and even political language.

For many women, lad culture was retrograde, a backlash against feminism's gains. But it also sparked response: women's magazines like Cosmopolitan and Just 17 pushed back with their own blend of sexuality and empowerment, and campaigns against Page 3 gained momentum. The clash between lad culture and Girl Power captured Britain's cultural contradictions.

The Ladettes and the Limits of Liberation

The 90s didn't just bring lad culture; it also gave rise to the "ladette." Figures like Zoe Ball, Sara Cox, and Denise Van Outen drank pints, swore on air, and smoked in public with the same unapologetic bravado as their male counterparts. To some, it was liberation, women claiming the right to misbehave. To others, it was a media caricature that trivialised feminism. The ladette era highlighted a cultural contradiction: women were more visible and powerful in music, media, and politics, yet still judged by double standards when they stepped outside traditional roles.

When America Came to Tea: Friends and US TV Imports

British viewers in the 1990s didn't just watch homegrown culture; they devoured American imports. Friends, which debuted in 1994, became a fixture of Friday nights and shaped how young Britons thought about relationships, fashion, and coffee shops. Alongside The X-Files, Frasier, and The Simpsons, US shows dominated schedules. The result was a cultural cross-pollination: Britain exported Britpop and Cool Britannia, while importing sitcoms and drama that made Starbucks and Manhattan loft apartments feel strangely familiar.

Cool Britannia

By the late 1990s, "Cool Britannia" had become shorthand for Britain's cultural confidence. Designers like Alexander McQueen and Stella McCartney took fashion global. Artists like Damien Hirst and Tracey Emin made shockwaves at the Turner Prize. Oasis played Knebworth to 250,000 fans over two nights.

Tony Blair's New Labour embraced it all. Musicians and fashion designers were invited to Downing Street receptions. The Union Jack, once a symbol of far-right nationalism, was rebranded as pop-culture chic. For a moment, Britain felt like the centre of the cultural world again.

Yet Cool Britannia's limits were clear. For every Tracey Emin in the art world, there were dozens of male-dominated bands. For every Girl Power anthem, lad mags shouted louder. The cultural renaissance was real, but it was uneven, reflecting the same contradictions seen in politics and the economy.

Eh-Oh! Teletubbies and Kids' Culture (1997)

Children's TV went global with the launch of Teletubbies in 1997. The brightly coloured, babbling creatures delighted toddlers and horrified some parents, who debated whether the show was genius or gibberish. Exported to over 100 countries, it was a reminder that culture wasn't just for teenagers or adults. The merchandising boom, toys, clothes, lunchboxes, also signalled a new era where children's culture became big business, shaping everything from playground chatter to Christmas shopping lists.

Harry Potter and the New Reading Culture (1997)

Amid the guitars and girl power of the 90s, another cultural giant emerged quietly in 1997: Harry Potter and the Philosopher's Stone. Written by J.K. Rowling in Edinburgh cafés, the story of the boy wizard became a publishing sensation. Midnight book launches, children reading on buses, adults sneaking fantasy novels on the Tube, Harry Potter revived the idea that books could be mass cultural events. It also turned Britain into the centre of a global literary empire, with Rowling herself becoming one of the most recognisable women of the decade.

WHY IT MATTERED

The culture of the 1990s reshaped Britain's image at home and abroad. Britpop and the Spice Girls made British music a global export worth billions. Cinema put Sheffield and Edinburgh alongside Notting Hill and Hollywood. Fashion and art set global trends.

But the decade also revealed tensions: women demanded a greater voice, but laddishness roared back. Female artists and musicians broke through but still fought against marginalisation. Girl Power may have been pop packaging, but it helped a generation of girls believe they belonged on the stage, not just in the audience.

Culture in the 1990s was noisy, contradictory, and impossible to ignore. It gave Britain swagger but also showed that cultural revolutions are always contested.

MINI TIMELINE – Culture

COOL BRITANNIA AND BEYOND

1991 – Bryan Adams' "(Everything I Do) I Do It for You" tops UK charts for 16 weeks, a record still standing

1992 – Whitney Houston's I Will Always Love You dominates global charts; Nirvana's Nevermind reshapes rock

1994 – Blur release Parklife; Loaded magazine launches; Four Weddings and a Funeral released

1995 – Oasis vs Blur "Battle of Britpop" (August); National Lottery arts funding begins; Criminal Justice Act targets raves

1996 – Spice Girls release Wannabe; Girl Power goes global; Trainspotting shocks audiences; Oasis play Knebworth; Friends lands on Channel 4

1997 – The Full Monty becomes international hit; Teletubbies launch; Harry Potter and the Philosopher's Stonepublished

1998 – Tracey Emin exhibits My Bed at Turner Prize; Shakespeare in Love wins Oscar; Fatboy Slim releases You've Come a Long Way, Baby

1999 – Notting Hill cements UK rom-com dominance; The Royle Family captures working-class life

4. SPORT AND NATIONAL PRIDE

ew decades stitched sport and national mood together like the 1990s. From Italia '90 to Euro '96, football had the nation singing again. Rugby Union turned professional, cricket lurched from scandal to triumph, and lottery money transformed Olympic prospects. Women's sport, long sidelined, began to push its way into the spotlight. Sport evolved into business, identity, and pride.

Italia '90: Tears, Tunes, and Togetherness

The decade began with heartbreak. At the 1990 World Cup in Italy, England's men reached their first semi-final since 1966. Paul Gascoigne's tears after his yellow card against West Germany, Chris Waddle's missed penalty in the shootout, and Pavarotti's soaring aria became national memories. Though England lost, the tournament sparked a cultural moment. Football, bruised by hooliganism and devastated by the Hillsborough disaster of 1989, became safe to love again.

For women, the contrast was stark. England's women's

football team, though formally recognised by the FA in 1993, had virtually no funding and little media coverage. The FA had only lifted its 50-year ban on women's football in 1971. Italia '90 showed football's emotional power; women players could only watch, waiting for their turn to be taken seriously.

THE PREMIER LEAGUE Revolution (1992)

Two years later, football changed forever. In 1992, the First Division broke away to form the Premier League. Sky Sports bought the rights for £304 million over five years, installed Monday Night Football with Richard Keys and Andy Gray, and drenched the game in razzmatazz. Suddenly, footballers weren't just athletes; they were millionaires, celebrities, and global brands.

Attendances rose from 9.7 million in the first season (1992–93) to 11.6 million by 1997–98, stadiums modernised after the Taylor Report, and families returned. The Premier League turned into an international product, with Manchester United dominating under Sir Alex Ferguson and David Beckham becoming the poster boy of a new sporting age.

Meanwhile, women's football struggled for scraps. The Women's FA Cup Final wasn't televised regularly, and players juggled jobs with training. Yet grassroots participation grew steadily, a slow burn that would one day fuel the Women's Super League and Lionesses' triumphs decades later.

EURO '96: Football's Coming Home

If Italia '90 reopened the door, Euro '96 blew it wide. Hosted in England from 8 to 30 June 1996, the tournament had everything: penalty drama, Paul Gascoigne's flick-and-volley against Scotland, and Baddiel & Skinner's Three Lions anthem declaring "football's coming home."

England's semi-final loss to Germany on penalties at Wembley was gutting, but the mood was electric. Wembley thrummed with colour, pubs overflowed, and "It's coming home" entered the national vocabulary. Total attendance reached 1.2 million across the tournament.

Yet women's football was excluded from the party. UEFA still treated it as a side project, and English media gave it barely a mention. The disparity was glaring, men's football boomed, women's football fought for recognition.

Manchester United's Treble (1999)

The defining club moment of the decade came in May 1999, when Manchester United completed an unprecedented Treble. Premier League, FA Cup, and Champions League. In Barcelona, United trailed Bayern Munich until stoppage time, when Teddy Sheringham and Ole Gunnar Solskjær scored in dramatic succession. It was the crowning moment of Sir Alex Ferguson's reign and symbolised English football's rebirth as a global spectacle.

Rugby Union Goes Professional (1995)

In 1995, Rugby Union finally turned professional after the World Cup in South Africa, immortalised by Nelson Mandela handing the trophy to Francois Pienaar. In Britain, clubs began paying players openly, transforming the sport from its amateur traditions.

For women, the breakthrough came slowly. The first Women's Rugby World Cup had been held in 1991, but with little fanfare or funding. By the mid-90s, the England women's team was competing at world level, though often self-funding travel and equipment. While male players cashed in on professionalism, female players continued to play for pride and passion.

WOMEN'S RUGBY **World Cup Triumph (1994)**

While the men's game only turned professional in 1995, England's women quietly made history the year before. In 1994, they won the Women's Rugby World Cup, defeating the USA in the final. The victory barely made the back pages, but it was a landmark: proof that women could not only play rugby at the highest level but win on the world stage. Two decades later, the Red Roses would become a powerhouse, their roots firmly planted in the quiet triumph of the 1990s.

CRICKET'S CONTRASTS

Cricket lurched between glory and shame. The men's team struggled in Tests, embarrassed by Australia and rocked by match-fixing scandals abroad. Yet county cricket thrived, and stars like Darren Gough and Michael Atherton inspired loyalty among fans.

In women's cricket, quiet history was made. England women, led by Karen Smithies, won the 1993 World Cup on home soil at Lord's, a landmark victory almost invisible in the mainstream press. It was a reminder that women's sport often triumphed in silence, achieving excellence without recognition or reward.

THE LOTTERY EFFECT **(1994 Onwards)**

In 1994, the National Lottery launched, and with it came a new funding stream for sport. Money flowed into grass-roots facilities and elite training through Sport England and

UK Sport. Athletics, cycling, rowing, and swimming all bene-fitted. Initial sports funding was £58.5 million annually from 1997.

For women, this was transformative. Sports long ignored by sponsors suddenly had proper investment, opening path-ways for female Olympians who would dominate the 2000s and beyond. The foundation was laid for Britain's later Olympic success, particularly from Beijing 2008 onwards.

Icons and Role Models

The 1990s created sporting icons who transcended their sports. David Beckham bent free kicks and married a Spice Girl, uniting football and pop culture in ways previously unimaginable.

In tennis, Tim Henman gave British fans hope at Wimble-don, carrying the flag to four semi-finals between 1998 and 2002 and inspiring "Henman Hill." He never won the title, but his polite, fist-pumping determination made him a household name. Yet Henman's rise often overshadowed the women's game, where equally compelling stories unfolded.

Steffi Graf's dominance stretched into the 1990s, with Wimbledon wins in 1991, 1992, 1993, 1995 and 1996, while Martina Hingis became the youngest-ever Wimbledon champion at 16 in 1997. For British fans, Jana Novotná's tearful collapse in the 1993 final against Graf, when she was comforted by the Duchess of Kent on Centre Court, was one of Wimbledon's most poignant moments. By the mid-90s, an additional force was emerging as Venus Williams thundered onto the scene, quickly followed by Serena, setting up the era of the Williams sisters that would transform women's tennis.

British athletics shone brightly. Linford Christie won Olympic gold in the 100m at Barcelona in 1992, becoming one of the fastest men on the planet, though later facing controversy over drug allegations. Sally Gunnell added 400m hurdles gold at the same Games, then followed up with World and European titles, completing a clean sweep. Colin Jackson set a world record in the 110m hurdles in 1993 that stood for over a decade. Later in the decade, Kelly Holmes began her ascent, winning European and Commonwealth medals that set the stage for her Olympic glory in the 2000s. Denise Lewis also emerged as a future star, winning heptathlon bronze in Atlanta 1996.

For the first time, schoolgirls had female sporting heroes to look up to on TV, even if coverage remained patchy. But sponsorship was still male-dominated, and women's achievements were celebrated briefly before being pushed off the back pages. These athletes nevertheless gave Britain a proud presence on the global stage, inspiring a new generation to lace up spikes, pick up rackets, and dream.

PARALYMPIC PRIDE

The 1990s also saw Britain's Paralympians rise to prominence. Tanni Grey-Thompson won four gold medals at the 1992 Barcelona Games and another in Atlanta 1996, becoming a household name and role model for disabled athletes. Wheelchair racing, swimming, and cycling successes helped push Paralympic sport closer to the mainstream, though television coverage remained limited compared to the Olympics.

For disabled children, seeing athletes like Grey-Thompson dominate on the world stage was transformative, offering visibility and proof that physical disabilities did not limit sporting excellence. The seeds of London 2012's Paralympic success were sown in this era, as Britain began to embrace the idea of inclusive sporting pride.

. . .

Lennox Lewis: Heavyweight Champion

British boxing also found a global hero in Lennox Lewis, who became undisputed heavyweight champion in the late 1990s. Calm, calculating, and clinical, Lewis was the antithesis of the brash Mike Tyson, yet he defeated Tyson in 2002 after a decade of dominance. In the 1990s, Lewis carried British boxing onto the world stage, a reminder that Britain's sporting pride extended well beyond football.

Damon Hill and Formula 1 Glory

Formula 1 also gave Britain moments of both tragedy and triumph. Damon Hill, son of double world champion Graham Hill, became the nation's racing hero after stepping into the spotlight in the early 1990s.

In 1994, Hill was thrust into the role of team leader at Williams following the death of Ayrton Senna at Imola, one of the sport's darkest days. That year's championship ended in bitter controversy, with Hill narrowly losing out to Michael Schumacher after a notorious collision in Adelaide.

Undeterred, Hill battled Schumacher for much of the decade, embodying resilience and determination. In 1996, he finally claimed the Formula 1 World Championship, the first son of a world champion to do so. His victory was celebrated across Britain, with Hill hailed as a dignified, understated champion in contrast to the sport's glamour and politics.

His success kept Britain's long tradition in motorsport alive, bridging the gap between Nigel Mansell's 1992 title and the dominance of Lewis Hamilton in the 2000s and 2010s. For a summer, Hill made Formula 1 feel like a national pastime, uniting casual fans with petrolheads in front of the TV every other Sunday.

· · ·

WHY IT MATTERED

Sport in the 1990s became big business and mass entertainment. The Premier League transformed English football into a global product worth billions, and Manchester United's Treble showed its reach. Euro '96 gave the nation a soundtrack and a sense of belonging that still echoes today. Rugby Union abandoned amateurism, cricket lurched between scandal and quiet triumph, and lottery funding reshaped Britain's Olympic future. Damon Hill carried British motorsport to world championship glory, Lennox Lewis dominated heavyweight boxing, and Paralympians like Tanni Grey-Thompson made disability sport visible and inspirational on a new scale.

But the decade also revealed the gender gap in stark terms. Men's sport became rich, professional, and central to national identity, while women's sport survived on dedication, part-time sacrifice, and fleeting headlines. Yet seeds were planted: the Lionesses, Red Roses, Wimbledon champions, Paralympic heroes, and Olympic stars of later decades all grew out of the persistence and groundwork of the 1990s.

In the end, sport in the 90s wasn't just about winning or losing, it was about who got to play, who got seen, and who got paid. And though the decade exposed deep inequalities, it also laid the foundations for a fairer, more inclusive sporting future that Britain would begin to embrace in the 2000s and beyond.

MINI TIMELINE – **Sport**

1990 – Italia '90: England reach World Cup semi-final

1992 – Premier League launches with £304m Sky Sports deal; Linford Christie wins Olympic 100m gold; Tanni Grey-Thompson wins 4 Paralympic golds

1993 – England women win Cricket World Cup at

Lord's; FA formally recognises women's football; Jana Novotná's tearful Wimbledon final

1994 – England women win Rugby World Cup; National Lottery launches, sport funding begins; Ayrton Senna dies at Imola GP, Damon Hill becomes Williams' lead driver

1995 – Rugby Union goes professional globally

1996 – Euro '96 hosted in England; "Three Lions (Football's Coming Home)" becomes anthem; Denise Lewis wins Olympic bronze in heptathlon; Tanni Grey-Thompson adds Paralympic golds in Atlanta; Damon Hill wins F1 World Championship

1997 – Lottery sports funding reaches £58.5m annually; Martina Hingis becomes youngest Wimbledon champion at 16

1999 – Manchester United complete historic Treble

5. TECHNOLOGY AND THE DIGITAL DAWN

⁕

*T*he 1990s were the decade that Britain went online. At the start of the decade, few households had a computer. By the end, email addresses were scrawled on business cards, mobiles were buzzing in handbags, and "dot-com" had become shorthand for the future. The Digital Dawn was clunky and slow, dial-up modems screeching, floppy disks corrupting, but it reshaped how Britons worked, played, and connected.

THE PC in the Living Room

In 1995, Microsoft released Windows 95 on August 24 , turning the PC into something far more approachable. The launch blitz even licensed the Rolling Stones' Start Me Up to hype the new Start button. Homes and schools started buying beige desktops with bulky CRT monitors.

By the late 1990s, the National Grid for Learning (1998) and the BBC's Bitesize revision site (1998) pushed digital resources into classrooms, while Tesco Computers for Schools (1992 onwards) filled IT suites via supermarket vouchers. Children were growing up digital though tentatively, awkwardly, but also irreversibly.

Women, often pigeonholed as secretaries in earlier computing eras, began using PCs for project management, teaching resources, and design. Typing pools gave way to Word and Excel, which put clerical power directly into people's hands. But stereotypes persisted: IT departments remained heavily male-dominated, and advertising rarely pictured women as decision-makers.

Dial-Up Dreams

For those who could afford a modem, the internet trickled into British homes in the mid-90s. Early adopters logged on via CompuServe and AOL, but the real breakthrough was Freeserve (launched September 1998), offering "free" access with only local call charges. By 1999, around 20% of UK households had home internet access.

Web pages loaded line by line, email felt miraculous, and search engines like Yahoo! and Ask Jeeves became gateways to knowledge. The World Wide Web, invented by Tim Berners-Lee at CERN, had gone public in 1991, but widespread adoption was slow and expensive.

Chatrooms, forums, and message boards created new social spaces. The internet was liberating for isolated individuals, but it also became a new frontier for harassment, with trolling and online abuse already emerging.

Mobile Mania

At the start of the decade, mobile phones were bricks for bankers and estate agents. By the end, they were everywhere. The arrival of pay-as-you-go in 1996 democratised mobile access beyond business users and the wealthy.

Late-90s icons included the Nokia 8110, the "banana phone" made famous by The Matrix (1999) and the Nokia 6110 (1997–98), which popularized the built-in Snake. Mobile penetration leapt to over 43 million subscriptions by 2000, up from virtually zero at the decade's start.

Mobiles changed dating (no more waiting by landlines), business (constant connectivity), and family life (parents could eventually track teenagers).

The First Text Message (1992)

On 3 December 1992, Neil Papworth, a 22-year-old British engineer for Vodafone, sent the world's first text: two words, "Merry Christmas." At the time, it seemed like a gimmick. Within a few years, it was a revolution. Texting became the preferred way for teenagers to talk, for couples to flirt, and for parents to check in with their kids.

Gaming Goes Global

In September 1995, the Sony PlayStation launched in Europe, reshaping leisure. Games like Gran Turismo, Tekken, and Tomb Raider (1996) created a generation of gamers. PC gaming flourished too, with Doom (1993), Command & Conquer (1995), and later The Sims (2000) designed by Will Wright and embraced especially by women for its open-ended storytelling.

Crucially, the 90s gave us Lara Croft. Designed by a mostly male team at Core Design, she was both groundbreaking and problematic, a heroine in a male-dominated industry, but also hyper-sexualised with anatomically impossible proportions. For many girls, though, Lara was the first time they saw themselves as the centre of the adventure, not the sidekick.

. . .

From **VHS to DVD (1996–98)**

For most of the 1990s, home entertainment still meant rewinding VHS tapes. But in 1997–98, DVDs arrived in Britain, promising sharper pictures, bonus features, and no need to rewind. At first, they were expensive luxuries, but by the decade's end they were replacing tapes in shops and living rooms. DVD players symbolised how quickly technology was moving: what felt cutting-edge in 1995 could feel outdated by 1999.

The Dot-Com Bubble

By the late 1990s, talk of the "information superhighway" was everywhere. Start-ups promised to revolutionise shopping, dating, and news. Britain had its own dot-com darlings, from Freeserve to Lastminute.com (founded in 1998 by Martha Lane Fox and Brent Hoberman). Lane Fox became one of Britain's best-known digital pioneers, her visibility challenging the idea that tech was only for men in hoodies.

The bubble would burst spectacularly in 2000–2001, but the seeds of the modern digital economy had been planted. Many of the failed dot-coms had the right ideas, just the wrong timing.

Media, Music, and New Frontiers

Technology blurred into culture. CDs had largely replaced vinyl and cassettes by the mid-90s, offering perfect digital sound. Then MP3s and Napster arrived in 1999, disrupting the music industry. Peer-to-peer file sharing allowed teenagers to build vast digital libraries, often illegally.

Television also exploded. Sky Digital launched in October 1998, and ONdigital followed in November, heralding the multi-channel era. The BBC launched BBC Online in April 1997, bringing public service content to the web.

Women were central as both consumers and creators. Teenage girls were among the earliest digital downloaders, curating pop libraries track by track. Female journalists and presenters, from Martha Kearney on News 24 to Gaby Roslin on The Big Breakfast, helped normalise women's voices in a changing media landscape.

WHY IT MATTERED

The Digital Dawn of the 1990s wasn't smooth or equal. Dial-up was slow, mobiles expensive, and the gender gap in tech careers persisted. But the decade normalised technology in daily life. By 2000, it was unthinkable not to have email, a mobile, or a computer.

The 1990s were clumsy, noisy, and often laughable in their tech dreams. But they set Britain on the path to a connected, mobile, digital society. Every time we scroll through smartphones that descended from those chunky Nokias or binge-watch Netflix over broadband that evolved from screeching dial-up, we're living the promise of the 1990s Digital Dawn.

MINI TIMELINE – Technology

1991 – World Wide Web opened to the public

1993 – First mainstream UK internet providers emerge; Mosaic makes the web visual

1995 – Windows 95 released (24 August); Sony PlayStation launches in UK (29 September)

1996 – Tomb Raider introduces Lara Croft; pay-as-you-go mobile phones launched

1997 – BBC Online launches; DVD hardware reaches UK shops

1998 – Google founded; Lastminute.com launched by Martha Lane Fox and Brent Hoberman; Freeserve brings free internet access; Sky Digital and ONdigital launch

1999 – Napster disrupts music industry; The Sims released; ~20% of UK households online; mobiles surge toward mass adoption

The Digital Dawn was Britain's awkward adolescence into the online age. It was the decade of screeching modems and pixelated graphics, but also the first-time technology felt personal, portable, and indispensable.

6. SCIENCE, HEALTH AND TRUST

$\mathcal{T}$he 1990s weren't just about politics, pop, and technology, they were also a decade when science and health repeatedly made headlines, often with a mix of fear, wonder, and controversy. Food scares shook public trust. Genetics promised a future of medical miracles. Cloning and GM foods forced moral debates into the supermarket aisle. HIV/AIDS, once taboo, became part of the public conversation. And for the first time, climate science entered mainstream politics. Britain entered the decade with optimism about science, but left it grappling with questions about trust, ethics, and who really benefited from breakthroughs.

BSE AND SHATTERED Confidence (1996)

The BSE crisis, better known as "mad cow disease," became one of the decade's darkest health scares. When in March 1996 the UK government admitted that BSE could be transmitted to humans in the form of vCJD, consumer confidence collapsed. Families stopped eating beef, supermarkets pulled products, and exports were banned across Europe. Farming communities faced devastation.

The government's reassurances that beef was safe rang hollow, especially after years of denial and mismanagement. The crisis revealed a wider problem: trust in official advice about food safety. Mothers making family meals, traditionally tasked with feeding households, suddenly faced terrifying uncertainty about something as ordinary as a Sunday roast.

GM FOODS AND THE "FRANKENSTEIN" Panic

Hot on the heels of BSE came a new controversy: genetically modified foods. By the mid-to-late 1990s, supermarkets were importing GM soya and maize from the US, and tabloids screamed warnings about "Frankenstein foods." Campaigners staged supermarket protests, while activists ripped up test crops in fields.

Scientists insisted GM foods were safe and potentially essential to future food security. But for many Britons, still scarred by BSE, reassurance was not enough. The GM debate highlighted a new reality: food wasn't just about nutrition, it was about trust in science, government, and corporations.

THE HUMAN GENOME PROJECT (1990–1999)

Behind the noise of food scares, one of the most ambitious scientific undertakings in history was unfolding. Launched in 1990, the Human Genome Project aimed to map all of human DNA. British scientists, especially in Cambridge and at the Sanger Centre, were central to the effort.

The implications were staggering. Mapping the genome promised new treatments for cancer, heart disease, and inherited disorders. Yet it also raised troubling ethical questions: who would own genetic data? Would employers or insurers discriminate based on DNA? Would "designer babies" become a reality? For women, the promise was double-edged: genetics might improve reproductive health and cancer care, but it also risked reducing their bodies to sites of scientific experimentation.

By 1999, researchers announced that a working draft of the human genome was close to completion, a scientific milestone that hinted at the century ahead.

DOLLY THE SHEEP (1996)

In February 1996, scientists at the Roslin Institute in Scotland unveiled Dolly the Sheep, the first mammal cloned from an adult cell. For some, it was proof of human ingenuity; for others, it was the stuff of dystopian nightmares. Could humans be cloned next? Should they be?

The debate revealed how the public often processed science through spectacle. Dolly appeared on magazine covers, cartoons, and political jokes. The ethical questions were profound, but the coverage often sensationalised the story. For Britain, Dolly was both a symbol of cutting-edge research and a reminder that science could move faster than society's ability to decide its limits.

AIDS Awareness and Changing Attitudes

In the 1980s, HIV/AIDS was shrouded in fear and stigma. By the 1990s, the conversation began to change. Medical advances, new drug therapies (antiretroviral "cocktail" treatments) introduced in 1996 transformed HIV from a near-certain death sentence into a manageable condition for many. Campaigners shifted focus from fear to awareness, demanding education, research, and compassion.

Princess Diana played a pivotal role. Her decision to shake hands with AIDS patients without gloves in the late 1980s carried into the 90s, with her continued advocacy helping to break down stigma. LGBTQ+ activists, many of them women, campaigned tirelessly for recognition and support. For Britain, AIDS awareness was a test of empathy: could a society frightened by difference embrace a common humanity?

The Climate Awakening

Science in the 1990s was not only about medicine and genetics; it was also about the planet itself. The Rio Earth Summit of 1992 brought global leaders together to discuss sustainable development and climate change. For the first time, environmental science was not just for activists; it was on the political agenda.

By 1995, the Intergovernmental Panel on Climate Change (IPCC) issued a landmark report stating there was a "discernible human influence" on global climate. Two years later, the Kyoto Protocol (1997) committed industrial nations, including Britain, to reducing greenhouse gas emissions. While targets were modest, the symbolism was immense: governments could no longer deny that climate change was real.

In everyday life, environmental awareness trickled into recycling bins, CFC-free aerosols, and early "green consumerism." The ozone hole over Antarctica, discovered in the 1980s, began to show signs of recovery in the 90s thanks to the Montreal Protocol phasing out ozone-depleting chemicals.

. . .

The NHS in Transition

Science and health in the 1990s were not confined to laboratories or headlines, they were lived daily in GP surgeries and hospital wards. The NHS, founded on the ideals of universal care, struggled with rising demand, chronic underfunding, and public frustration. John Major's Conservative government introduced the "internal market" reforms of 1991, creating a purchaser–provider split that turned health authorities into buyers of care and hospitals into competing "trusts." The language of business entered the wards, and many staff felt the system was becoming fragmented.

By the mid-1990s, waiting lists and delays dominated headlines. The public worried about whether the NHS could cope, and stories of cancelled operations and long waits for cancer treatment chipped away at confidence.

When Labour came to power in 1997, Tony Blair promised to save the NHS. His government launched the "24-hour pledge" that every patient would be able to see a GP within a day and injected new funding streams, some from the newly launched National Lottery who supported some specific projects such as healthy living centres. But reforms also expanded managerial layers, and debates raged over whether the NHS was becoming more responsive or more bureaucratic.

For women, the backbone of the NHS as nurses, carers, cleaners, and increasingly doctors, these reforms often meant more paperwork, more pressure, and more juggling of underfunded services. Yet the NHS remained deeply trusted by the public, even as trust in governments' ability to manage it wavered.

. . .

Why It Mattered

The science and health debates of the 1990s shaped more than policies; they shaped trust. BSE and GM foods revealed how quickly confidence in government could collapse. Dolly the Sheep and the Human Genome Project showed that scientific possibility outpaced ethical consensus. Climate change awareness showed that science was no longer just local or national; it was global. AIDS awareness proved that stigma could be challenged, but only through sustained activism and human connection. The NHS became a mirror of that trust: still beloved but caught between ideals of care and realities of reform.

The legacy of the 1990s remains visible today. Every new food scare, from horse meat to pesticides, carries echoes of BSE. GM crops are still contested. Genetic science underpins modern medicine, but debates about privacy and ownership rage on. AIDS, though more treatable, continues to demand public awareness. Climate change, once a distant warning, is now an everyday crisis. The NHS is still debated, defended, and demanded. The decade taught Britain that science is never neutral; it is social, political, and deeply human.

Mini Timeline – Science, Health, and Trust

1990 – Human Genome Project launched

1991 – NHS "internal market" reforms introduced

1992 – Rio Earth Summit raises climate change to global politics

1993 – GM crop trials begin in the UK

1995 – IPCC states "discernible human influence" on climate

1996 – BSE crisis peaks; beef exports banned

1996 – Dolly the Sheep cloned in Scotland

1996 – New HIV/AIDS drug therapies transform survival rates

1997 – Campaigners escalate protests against "Frankenstein foods"; Kyoto Protocol agreed; Labour pledges GP access within 24 hours

1999 – Draft sequencing of the human genome nearly complete

7. SOCIAL SHIFTS AND EVERYDAY LIFE

*T*he 1990s were the decade when everyday life in Britain started to look recognisably modern. The corner shop gave way to the supermarket superstore, IKEA flat-packs replaced heirloom furniture, and takeaway coffee cups became the accessory of choice. Families were changing, women's work was reshaping households, and consumer culture was accelerating. Beneath the pop anthems and Cool Britannia slogans, the 1990s rewrote daily routines—often quietly, but permanently.

THE HIGH STREET Boom

Walk down a British high street in the mid-90s and you'd see the transformation accelerating. Chains expanded rapidly: Next, Topshop, HMV, and Virgin Megastores drew in young shoppers, while supermarkets grew into megastores, adding cafés, pharmacies, and petrol stations. IKEA, with its cheap, minimalist Swedish design, became a rite of passage for first homes and student flats.

The Sunday Trading Act (1994) allowed shops to open on

Sundays for the first time, fundamentally changing the rhythm of British life. What had once been a day of rest became another shopping opportunity. Out-of-town retail parks and shopping centres like the Trafford Centre (opened 1998) symbolised this new consumer age.

Shopping was increasingly about identity. Clothes, trainers, CDs - they weren't just purchases; they were cultural markers. Women, long positioned as primary consumers, were courted more aggressively than ever. Magazines like Elle and Cosmopolitan fuelled trends, while loyalty cards and "buy one get one free" deals made consumption feel like a savvy strategy.

The Coffee Cup Revolution

By the late 1990s, American-style coffee shops were everywhere. Starbucks arrived in London in 1998; Caffè Nero opened its first branch in 1997; while Costa Coffee, founded in 1971, expanded rapidly into the high street mainstream. The sight of commuters with takeaway lattes signalled a shift: Britain was no longer just a nation of tea drinkers. Coffee culture meant longer working hours, lunch meetings, and new social spaces that blurred work and leisure.

For women, cafés were more than convenience. They became spaces for mothers to meet with prams, students to revise, and professionals to network outside male-dominated offices. The disposable cup became a new symbol of busyness, sophistication, and independence.

FAMILY AND HOME Life

Family life was in flux. Divorce rates peaked in the mid-90s at 13.8 per 1,000 married couples. Single-parent families became more visible, with 1.7 million lone-parent households by 1997, often headed by women juggling work and childcare. The "nuclear family" model still dominated advertising and political rhetoric, but reality was more diverse.

Women entered the workforce in record numbers, reaching 68% participation by 1997 many part-time, often in retail or service work. Two incomes became the norm, not the exception, but childcare provision lagged. Only under Labour after 1997 did childcare become a political priority, with the National Childcare Strategy (1998) aiming to create 900,000 new childcare places.

At home, technology crept into living rooms: bigger TVs, home PCs, and games consoles. The "family meal" often moved from the dining table to the sofa in front of Friends, EastEnders, or the evening news. Video rental shops like Blockbuster became weekend rituals, with Friday night queues stretching out the door.

Food, Fitness, and Body Image

The 1990s were obsessed with body image and contradictory messages about food and fitness. Low-fat diets dominated, Weight Watchers memberships soared, and celebrity workout videos (from Mr Motivator to Jane Fonda knock-offs) filled living rooms. The "heroin chic" look popularised by Kate Moss sparked fierce debates about fashion's promotion of unhealthy body ideals.

Women bore the brunt of this culture. Teenage girls leafed through Sugar and Just 17 magazines filled with diet tips alongside boyband posters. At the same time, the gym and aerobics craze gave women new spaces for fitness and confidence. Chain gyms like David Lloyd Leisure and Virgin Active expanded rapidly. The tension between empowerment and pressure was constant and unresolved.

. . .

THE LADETTE LIFESTYLE

The mid-1990s saw the rise of the "ladette" women who partied hard, drank pints, smoked in clubs, and swore just as freely as men. Media figures like Zoe Ball and Sara Cox embodied the trend, fronting TV and radio with brash confidence. In pubs and nightclubs, young women mirrored the laddish culture of their male peers, embracing freedom but also facing backlash. For some, it was liberation from the pressure to be "ladylike." For others, it was a double standard in disguise: men's wildness was cheeky, women's was reckless. The ladette era reflected broader social shifts, women taking up space in nightlife and media, but also highlighted how gender roles were still policed.

DIVERSITY IN DAILY LIFE

Britain's cities grew more multicultural through the 1990s. Asian and Afro-Caribbean communities reshaped food culture, bringing curries, jerk chicken, and halal butchers into the mainstream. Chicken tikka masala was famously dubbed Britain's "national dish" by Foreign Secretary Robin Cook in 2001, but its popularity was cemented in the 1990s.

At the same time, racism and inequality persisted. The murder of Stephen Lawrence (1993) and the Macpherson Report (1999) exposed institutional racism in the police and highlighted daily prejudice faced by Black Britons. For women of colour, inequalities were multiplied, navigating sexism and racism in both workplaces and communities, often with less support than white women or men of colour.

WORK-LIFE BALANCE AND THE "FLEXIBLE" ECONOMY

The 1990s introduced a new buzzword: flexibility. Zero-hour contracts, agency work, and temping grew rapidly as employers sought to reduce costs and increase adaptability. For employers, it meant efficiency. For workers, often women, it meant insecurity disguised as opportunity.

Many women patched together part-time jobs with child-care responsibilities, often working evenings, weekends, or school hours. While this allowed some independence, it also entrenched the gender pay gap, around 17% for full-time workers. Men dominated senior roles in finance and tech, while women filled the checkout lines, call centres, and care jobs.

The average working week lengthened, particularly for professional couples. The phrase "work-life balance" entered common usage, though achieving it remained elusive for most families.

Religion, Sexuality, and Identity

Church attendance declined steadily throughout the decade, but faith communities remained important in many areas, particularly among immigrant populations. Simultaneously, LGBTQ+ visibility grew despite Section 28, the law banning the "promotion" of homosexuality in schools, introduced in 1988 and not repealed until 2003.

Soap operas like Brookside broke ground with the UK's first lesbian kiss (1994), reshaping how sexuality was portrayed in everyday life. The age of consent for gay men was lowered from 21 to 18 in 1994, though full equality at 16 wouldn't come until 2001. Campaigners staged high-profile protests against Section 28 throughout the 1990s, challenging stigma in schools and local councils.

Women were at the forefront of these shifts, both as campaigners for change and as symbols of cultural anxiety.

Madonna's global influence, the Spice Girls' Girl Power, and debates about ladettes all challenged traditional expectations of femininity in daily life.

EVERYDAY AMERICA: **Friends and Sitcom Imports**

Daily life in the 1990s Britain wasn't just shaped by what happened at home; it was influenced by what came through the television. American sitcoms like Friends (1994), Frasier (1993), and The Simpsons (1990 on UK TV) became part of the furniture. They shaped language ("we were on a break!"), fashion (Rachel haircuts, coffee-shop chic), and even leisure habits, as young Britons sought out Starbucks-style cafés instead of pubs. The sitcom invasion was more than entertainment; it was a subtle reshaping of British social life, blending homegrown routines with imported ideals of friendship, humour, and aspiration.

LEISURE AND HOLIDAYS

The 1990s also reshaped how Britons spent their leisure time. Package holidays boomed, with low-cost airlines beginning to disrupt the industry. Ryanair, once a small Irish carrier, rebranded in 1995 as a no-frills airline and pioneered the cheap-flight model that would revolutionise European travel. For the first time, families and groups of friends could afford weekends away in Spain or city breaks in Prague.

Ibiza and Magaluf became rites of passage for young clubbers, their reputations fuelled by the rise of superclubs and the explosion of dance music culture. "Brits abroad" stereotypes, lager, sunburn, and loudness, became tabloid staples, but so did stories of affordable adventure.

Closer to home, new leisure options transformed weekends. Center Parcs, which opened in Sherwood Forest in 1987, expanded in the 1990s with new sites at Longleat (1993) and Elveden (1994). Theme parks like Alton Towers and Thorpe Park modernised with new rollercoasters, making day trips more thrilling.

Domestic leisure was also about staying in. Video rentals from Blockbuster, meals from fast-food chains, and nights out at multiplex cinemas meant that leisure was increasingly commodified and standardised.

EDUCATION AND ASPIRATION

Education also shifted profoundly in the 1990s. The National Curriculum, introduced in 1988, was bedded in and expanded, with pupils sitting SATs at ages 7, 11, and 14 by the mid-90s. For parents, the tests became a new source of dinner-table stress.

Secondary schools faced league tables and inspections, putting performance into the public eye. By 1997, school uniforms, homework diaries, and Ofsted visits were familiar parts of everyday life.

Higher education expanded dramatically. The proportion of young people going to university doubled across the decade, supported by the expansion of polytechnics into universities in 1992. But the change came with a cost: in 1998, the government introduced tuition fees for the first time, and student loans replaced maintenance grants.

For women, this expansion meant greater access to degrees and careers previously closed off. Yet the burden of debt was new, and many graduates entered a flexible, insecure job market rather than the secure professions their parents had known.

. . .

Why It Mattered

The everyday Britain of the 1990s feels strangely familiar today. Chain stores, coffee shops, IKEA furniture, and blended families they all became normal then. Multiculturalism transformed food, fashion, and language, even as racism and discrimination persisted.

The contradictions of the decade are clear in hindsight. Consumerism offered choice and empowerment, but also new pressures and inequalities. The "flexible" economy gave opportunity and insecurity in equal measure. Sunday shopping meant convenience but also the erosion of traditional rhythms. Education opened doors but introduced debt. Package holidays and cheap flights opened the continent but also created a new culture of consumption abroad.

The 1990s taught Britain to live with these tensions, and we still do.

Mini Timeline – Everyday Life

1991 – Supermarket chains expand into megastores with cafés and services

1993 – Divorce rates peak; Stephen Lawrence murdered; Center Parcs Longleat opens

1994 – Sunday Trading Act allows shops to open Sundays; Brookside shows UK's first lesbian kiss; age of consent for gay men lowered to 18; Center Parcs Elveden opens

1995 – Kate Moss "heroin chic" fashion controversy peaks; Ryanair relaunches as a no-frills airline

1997 – Female workforce participation reaches 68%; 1.7m lone-parent households; Caffè Nero founded

1998 – Trafford Centre opens; National Childcare Strategy launched; Starbucks arrives in UK; tuition fees introduced for students

1999 – Macpherson Report finds police institutionally racist

The 1990s reshaped Britain not just in politics or culture, but in the small things: what we ate, how we shopped, where we studied, where we worked, where we travelled, and who we lived with. It was a decade when everyday life looked less like the past — and more like now.

8. DIVERSITY AND IDENTITY

$\mathcal{T}$he 1990s were a decade of shifting identities. Britain was becoming more visibly multicultural, more willing to debate race, gender, and sexuality, and more open to voices that had long been silenced. At the same time, the period exposed deep inequalities and prejudices. Diversity was celebrated in music, food, and fashion, but also contested in politics, schools, and the streets. If the 1980s had been a time of denial, the 1990s were the years Britain began, however unevenly, to confront itself.

THE STEPHEN LAWRENCE Case (1993)

On 22 April 1993, 18-year-old Stephen Lawrence was murdered in a racially motivated attack while waiting for a bus in Eltham, South London. The police investigation was incompetent from the start, marred by delays, assumptions, and indifference. His parents, Doreen and Neville Lawrence, refused to let the case fade into obscurity.

Their campaign became one of the defining civil rights struggles of modern Britain. Women were at its heart: Doreen Lawrence's dignity, persistence, and articulate demands for justice gave the case national and international attention. Anti-racism campaigners, many of them women, built coalitions that forced Parliament and police to act.

The Macpherson Report, published in February 1999 after a public inquiry, concluded that the Metropolitan Police was "institutionally racist" a phrase that shook the establishment and entered everyday discourse. The report made 70 recommendations for reform and fundamentally changed how Britain understood racism: not just individual prejudice, but systemic discrimination embedded in institutions.

The Lawrence case transformed debates on race, justice, and policing. It exposed the daily realities of racism faced by Black Britons and forced white Britain to admit that diversity was not just about celebration it required systemic change. The case continues to resonate today, with Gary Dobson and David Norris finally convicted in 2012 after changes to double jeopardy laws.

IMMIGRATION AND MULTICULTURALISM

The 1990s saw Britain's population become steadily more diverse. Immigration from South Asia, Africa, and the Caribbean continued, while new arrivals came from Eastern Europe and the Middle East as political situations shifted. British cities grew more multicultural in food, language, and music.

Cultural hybridity became mainstream. Bhangra beats mixed into club tracks, chicken tikka masala gained recognition as a British dish, and Black British artists like Tricky and Goldie entered the charts. The Asian Underground emerged, with artists like Talvin Singh and Nitin

Sawhney blending traditional sounds with cutting-edge production.

But multiculturalism sparked a backlash. Far-right groups such as the BNP sought footholds in towns, and asylum seekers became scapegoats in political debates. The Conservative government's Asylum and Immigration Act (1996) restricted rights and support, fuelling tensions. Women from minority backgrounds often bore the brunt, navigating racism, sexism, and cultural expectations within their own communities while facing discrimination in jobs, housing, and public services.

FAITH, Community, and Belonging

Religion played a quieter but still important role in shaping identity during the 1990s. Britain's growing Muslim communities-built mosques and cultural centres across cities, while Black churches flourished in London, Birmingham, and Manchester. Hindu temples and Sikh gurdwaras became key hubs.

For many immigrant families, faith communities provided stability in a rapidly changing society. But suspicion grew, media portrayals of Islam hardened, particularly after the Gulf War (1991) and conflicts in the Middle East, laying the foundations for Islamophobia that would intensify after 2001.

Women were often the most visible representatives of faith, wearing hijab in increasingly diverse workplaces, leading choirs, or organising community events. Their choices were frequently politicised in ways men's were not, making them symbols in wider debates about multiculturalism and belonging.

. . .

Section 28 and LGBTQ+ Rights

Since 1988, Section 28 of the Local Government Act had banned the "promotion" of homosexuality in schools. The law created a chilling effect: teachers avoided mentioning same-sex relationships, and LGBTQ+ students grew up in silence and isolation.

In the 1990s, protests intensified. Lesbian activists stormed BBC studios, chained themselves to railings, and marched at Pride events. LGBTQ+ culture gained visibility in soaps (Brookside aired the UK's first lesbian kiss in 1994), in magazines like Attitude (launched 1994), and in ever-growing Pride marches.

The age of consent for gay men was lowered from 21 to 18 in 1994, though equality at 16 wouldn't come until 2001. Section 28 remained law throughout the decade, not repealed until 2003 in England and Wales. Progress was slow and contested, but the activism of the 1990s laid the groundwork for later victories: equal age of consent, civil partnerships (2004), and eventually same-sex marriage (2013).

Women at the Forefront of Activism

Women were central to identity struggles of the 1990s. Doreen Lawrence's relentless campaign for justice exposed institutional racism. Lesbian activists led Section 28 protests. Black and Asian women organised locally around housing, education, and domestic violence, connecting personal struggles to political movements. Their activism broadened the definition of diversity, not just about race or sexuality in isolation, but about how gender, class, and identity overlapped.

Women, Work, and Identity

The 1990s saw women claim more space in public life, but identity politics highlighted how uneven progress was. White, middle-class women gained new career opportunities and political representation, while Black and Asian women still faced multiple barriers in pay, promotion, and visibility. Campaigns around equal pay, childcare, and maternity rights showed how gender inequalities cut across race and class lines.

The rise of the "ladette", epitomised by Zoe Ball or Sara Cox, reflected a new kind of female identity: women who drank, swore, and partied like men. To some, this was liberation from restrictive feminine ideals; to others, it felt like adopting male behaviours rather than reshaping expectations altogether.

Media Representation and Stereotypes

The 1990s saw both progress and problems in representation. British television began to showcase more diverse casts, with shows like Desmond's portraying Black British family life and Goodness Gracious Me satirising Asian British experiences. Yet news coverage often reinforced stereotypes, particularly around crime, immigration, and cultural practices.

Women of colour faced particular challenges, often either invisible or reduced to exotic stereotypes. Still, the rise of British Asian and Black British female artists, writers, and activists began to challenge these narratives. Identity was contested on-screen and off a constant negotiation between visibility, misrepresentation, and self-definition.

Why It Mattered

The 1990s forced Britain to confront diversity in ways

that could no longer be ignored or tokenised. Stephen Lawrence's murder revealed the costs of institutional racism and galvanised a generation of anti-racism campaigners. Section 28 protests highlighted LGBTQ+ resilience and the power of grassroots activism. Women's shifting roles showed both progress and the intersectional nature of inequality.

The decade didn't resolve these tensions, it exposed them and made them part of national conversation. But it created frameworks for understanding discrimination that still shape Britain today, from debates on policing to the visibility of Pride, from immigration policy to workplace equality. The battles of the 1990s laid foundations for later advances while revealing how much work remained to be done.

MINI TIMELINE – Diversity and Identity

1993 – Murder of Stephen Lawrence (22 April) sparks national campaign

1994 – Brookside airs UK's first lesbian kiss; age of consent for gay men lowered to 18; Attitude magazine launches

1996 – Asylum and Immigration Act restrict rights and support

1997 – First National Black Women's Conference held in London

1998 – Doreen Lawrence awarded OBE for campaigning

1999 – Macpherson Report declares Metropolitan Police "institutionally racist" (Feb)

The 1990s were messy, painful, and often contradictory, but they made identity part of the national conversation. Britain was no longer pretending to be one homogeneous thing; it was learning, haltingly, to live with many different identities and experiences within its borders.

9. TRAGEDY AND SHOCK

*T*he 1990s may be remembered for Britpop and Cool Britannia, but beneath the optimism lay moments of heartbreak and horror. From royal scandals to school shootings, from terrorist bombs to the sudden death of Diana, Princess of Wales, shocks that tested Britain's resilience and revealed deep vulnerabilities punctuated the decade. Women were often at the centre of these stories, as leaders, campaigners, symbols of grief, and agents of change.

THE QUEEN'S **Annus Horribilis (1992)**

In a rare moment of candour, Queen Elizabeth II described 1992 as her "annus horribilis" her horrible year. She was marking 40 years on the throne, but instead of jubilation came humiliation and crisis.

Royal marriages crumbled in spectacular fashion. Princess Anne divorced Mark Phillips, Andrew and Sarah Ferguson separated amid the "toe-sucking" scandal, and Charles and Diana's marriage collapsed under relentless media pressure and mutual infidelity. The publication of Andrew Morton's Diana: Her True Story (June 1992), based on secret interviews with the Princess, exposed dysfunction at the heart of the monarchy.

On 20 November 1992, a devastating fire ripped through Windsor Castle, destroying 115 rooms and costing millions to restore. When the Queen initially requested taxpayer money for repairs during a recession, public sympathy plummeted. The monarchy's approval ratings hit historic lows.

For the monarchy, 1992 marked a turning point. Female royals, in particular, were cast under harsh lights: Diana as the wronged "people's princess," Fergie as tabloid punchline, and the Queen herself criticised for being too remote.

THE JAMES BULGER Case (1993)

In February 1993, two-year-old James Bulger was abducted from a shopping centre in Bootle, Merseyside, by two ten-year-old boys. Hours later, his body was found by a railway line. The crime horrified Britain.

The idea that children could commit such an atrocity dominated headlines for months, sparking debates about childhood, innocence, and responsibility. Should ten-year-olds face adult justice? Were they products of their environment or innately violent? James's mother, Denise Fergus, became a tireless campaigner for victims' rights, ensuring that her son's name would not be forgotten.

The case remains one of the most haunting episodes in modern British criminal history and a reminder of how questions of morality, childhood, and justice can fracture public opinion.

THE DUNBLANE MASSACRE (1996)

On 13 March 1996, Britain was shaken by an act of unthinkable violence. Thomas Hamilton, a 43-year-old former scout leader, entered Dunblane Primary School in Scotland with four handguns. He killed 16 children and their teacher, Gwen Mayor, and injured 15 others before turning the gun on himself.

The massacre unleashed not just grief but determined anger. Parents launched the Snowdrop Campaign, demanding tougher gun laws. Ann Pearston, whose daughter Chloe was killed, became a leading voice. Parents led marches, gave interviews, and put relentless pressure on MPs.

Within two years, the campaign succeeded. The Firearms (Amendment) Acts of 1997 banned private ownership of most handguns, making the UK's gun laws among the strictest in the world. Dunblane was one of the most decisive policy shifts of the decade, driven by the moral force of ordinary families.

TERROR in the Cities

For much of the 1990s, IRA bombs continued to bring fear and devastation to British streets, even as peace negotiations progressed.

Warrington bombing (20 March 1993) injured 56 people and killed two young boys, Tim Parry (12) and Johnathan Ball (3). Their parents, Colin and Wendy Parry, became powerful voices for peace, establishing the Tim Parry Johnathan Ball Foundation for Peace.

The Bishopsgate bombing (24 April 1993) devastated London's financial district, causing almost £1 billion in damage, killing one person and injuring 44 people.

Manchester bombing (15 June 1996) saw a 3,300lb lorry bomb (the biggest bomb detonated in Britain since the

Second World War) injure over 200 and flatten much of the Arndale shopping centre. Miraculously, no one was killed because of the rapid evacuation of approximately 75,000 people.

THE OMAGH BOMBING (1998)

Just four months after the Good Friday Agreement, hope was shattered by the Real IRA's bombing of Omagh on 15 August 1998. A car bomb exploded in the town centre, killing 29 people, including one woman pregnant with twins, and injuring more than 200 people. It was the deadliest single atrocity of the Troubles.

The horror struck at a moment of fragile optimism, yet it galvanised rejection of violence. Families of victims became voices for peace. Omagh reminded Britain and Ireland that peace would always be tested but also that the appetite for it was stronger than terror.

THE DEATH of Diana (1997)

On 31 August 1997, Britain woke to shocking news that would define the decade's end: Princess Diana had died in a Paris car crash while being pursued by paparazzi. She was just 36.

The days that followed revealed a tidal wave of grief unlike anything in modern British history. Outside Kensington Palace, flowers piled waist-high. Men and women wept openly in the streets. For a country stereotyped as emotion-ally repressed, Diana's death unlocked a new language of grief.

The monarchy initially faltered. The Queen, at Balmoral with her grandsons, kept silent for six days. Her restraint was read as coldness in an age of rolling news. Public pressure, particularly from women writing letters and calling broadcasters, forced the Crown to respond. When the Queen finally addressed the nation on 5 September, she spoke not only as sovereign but as "a grandmother," acknowledging the human loss.

Diana's funeral on 6 September drew between 2 and 2.5 billion viewers worldwide and 31 million in the UK alone. The sight of her sons, William (15) and Harry (12), walking behind her coffin became one of the defining images of the decade.

Her legacy stretched beyond monarchy. Diana had campaigned for AIDS awareness, shaking hands with patients when others recoiled. Her walk through an Angolan minefield in January 1997 brought global attention to the landmine ban campaign. These images reshaped ideas of compassion and power.

THE MURDER of Jill Dando (1999)

On 26 April 1999, BBC presenter Jill Dando was shot dead outside her London home. As the face of Crimewatch, she was one of Britain's most trusted broadcasters, known for warmth and professionalism.

Her murder sparked one of the biggest police investigations in history. A suspect, Barry George, was convicted in 2001 but later acquitted; the case remains unsolved. Dando's death was more than a crime: it was a cultural rupture. The idea that such a beloved public figure could be killed on her doorstep unsettled Britain's sense of security as the decade closed.

MORE SHOCKS and Losses

The 1990s carried further traumas that tested national resilience:

Rail disasters: The Southall rail crash (1997) killed seven when a high-speed train passed a red signal; the Ladbroke Grove crash (1999) killed 31 and injured 417. Campaigns by bereaved families pushed through reforms in railway safety.

Hillsborough aftermath: Though the disaster occurred in 1989, the 1990s saw relentless campaigning for truth. Anne Williams, whose son Kevin, aged 15, died, became a leading campaigner, challenging the official narrative and pressing for new inquests until her death in 2013. A total of 97 people were killed as a result of the tragedy.

These tragedies reinforced a sense of vulnerability that modern Britain was not immune to horror, accident, or systemic failure.

Why It Mattered

The shocks of the 1990s revealed both vulnerability and resilience. The monarchy stumbled but adapted to an emotionally open age. Dunblane showed that citizens, led by determined individuals, could change laws when politicians hesitated. Terror attacks scarred cities but also fuelled peace efforts that culminated in the Good Friday Agreement. Diana's death redefined public mourning and shifted expectations of leaders forever.

Everyday individuals were central throughout: campaigners who turned grief into activism, community leaders who held society together, mourners who gave permission for public emotion, and reformers who transformed tragedy into change. They showed that in Britain's darkest moments, ordinary people often became extraordinary forces for reform.

The decade proved that Britain's identity wasn't only

shaped by Britpop or Cool Britannia. It was also forged in collective sorrow, trauma, and the determination to ensure such tragedies never happened again.

Mini Timeline – Tragedy and Shock

1992 – Queen's annus horribilis; Windsor Castle fire (20 Nov); royal marriages collapse

1993 – James Bulger murdered (12 Feb); IRA bombs Warrington (20 Mar) and Bishopsgate (24 Apr)

1996 – Dunblane massacre (13 Mar) leads to handgun ban; Manchester IRA bomb (15 Jun); EU bans British beef exports over BSE

1997 – Princess Diana dies (31 Aug); Southall rail crash kills 7 (19 Sep); Firearms Act bans most handguns

1998 – Omagh bombing kills 29 (15 Aug)

1999 – Jill Dando murdered (26 Apr); Ladbroke Grove rail crash kills 31 (5 Oct)

The 1990s taught Britain that tragedy could be both devastating and transformative. It was a decade in which grief became public, the people's voices carried moral authority for reform, and loss reshaped institutions. Out of sorrow came change and out of shock, a more resilient, emotionally honest society.

10. EUROPE AND THE WORLD

⁂

*T*he 1990s were a decade of global turbulence and transformation. New conflicts erupted in the Middle East and the Balkans, Europe moved towards closer union while Britain hesitated on the sidelines, and globalisation accelerated: cheap flights, satellite TV, and fast-food chains made the world feel smaller. For Britain, the decade was about redefining its place in Europe and on the world stage, often uneasily, always loudly.

THE END of the Cold War (1991)

The collapse of the Soviet Union in 1991 redrew the map of Europe and reshaped Britain's foreign policy. Suddenly the Cold War, which had dominated global politics for half a century, was over. For Britain, it meant reduced defence spending, new trade opportunities, and a search for relevance in a world no longer defined by East versus West. Former Soviet states looked westward, and NATO expanded, laying the groundwork for tensions that would resurface decades later. The end of the Cold War created both optimism and uncertainty: Britain was no longer a front-line power, but it still wanted to punch above its weight.

Maastricht and the European Question (1992–93)

The Maastricht Treaty, signed on 7 February 1992, created the European Union and set the course for a single currency. For John Major, getting it through Parliament became a nightmare that nearly destroyed his government. Eurosceptic MPs rebelled furiously, reducing the government's majority to single digits and forcing repeated votes.

The debate wasn't just about economics; it was about identity and sovereignty. Was Britain European, or forever semi-detached? Newspapers like The Sun and Daily Mail ran relentlessly anti-EU headlines, stoking scepticism that would later fuel Brexit. Major secured opt-outs from the single currency and the Social Chapter, but the divisions within the Conservative Party proved irreparable.

For women, European integration brought tangible benefits. EU directives strengthened maternity rights, workplace protections, and equal pay enforcement, pushing Britain to catch up on gender equality. Female MEPs such as Glenys Kinnock and Caroline Jackson put childcare, part-time workers' rights, and anti-discrimination onto the agenda. Yet the broader debate remained dominated by men in grey suits, masking the EU's practical impact on daily life.

Black Wednesday and the Euro Divide

When Britain crashed out of the Exchange Rate Mechanism on Black Wednesday (16 September 1992), hostility to integration deepened. While other countries prepared for the euro, Britain opted out, cementing a pattern of semi-detachment.

The humiliation hurt the government; the later recovery soothed markets but hardened a narrative that "Europe" meant loss of control.

The Channel Tunnel and Free Movement (1994 Onwards)

In 1994, the Channel Tunnel opened, a concrete symbol that Britain was physically tied to Europe even if politically ambivalent. Eurostar trains linked London with Paris and Brussels in hours. Budget airlines, Schengen's rise (which the UK opted out of), and Erasmus student exchanges knitted daily life more tightly to the continent: weekend breaks, semesters abroad, cross-Channel romances.

The Hong Kong Handover (1997)

On the night of 30 June 1997, Britain lowered its flag in Hong Kong for the last time. After 156 years of colonial rule, the territory was handed back to China under "one country, two systems." Prince Charles called it "the end of Empire." For Britain, it was both symbolic and practical: a final retreat from imperial dominance and the start of a more modest role as a European and global player. For Hong Kongers, it began a new and uncertain chapter whose consequences still echo.

War and Intervention

Britain's foreign policy was repeatedly tested by crisis.

The Gulf War (2 August 1990-28 February 1991) Britain joined the US-led coalition to expel Iraq from Kuwait. Women served in unprecedented numbers in support roles, and 24-hour news turned conflict into a live broadcast. The war showcased precision munitions and the power of television to shape public opinion.

The Rwandan Genocide (1994) While Britons debated Cool Britannia, horrific images arrived from Rwanda. In around 100 days, roughly 500,000 to 800,000 people were murdered and there was widespread sexual violence, with between 250,000 and 500,000 women raped. Britain, like much of the international community, stood by. Charities and campaigners demanded action; governments hesitated. Rwanda became a symbol of Western hypocrisy: promising "never again," then failing to act.

The Balkans (1992–99) Ethnic conflict in Bosnia and later Kosovo horrified Europe. Britain contributed peacekeepers and later joined NATO air campaigns. Bosnian women's groups exposed systematic rape as a weapon of war, forcing NATO and the UN to confront gendered crimes. British aid worker staffed camps, clinics, and convoys, bearing witness and saving lives.

The Kosovo War (1998-1999) Serbian forces drove ethnic Albanians from their homes; this time NATO intervened with air strikes. Tony Blair emerged as a champion of "humanitarian intervention," arguing Western powers had a duty to stop atrocities. The war was short but controversial, raising questions about sovereignty and international law. Kosovo foreshadowed the next decade: the promise and peril of interventionism.

Sierra Leone (2000) Just beyond the decade, UK forces' rapid intervention stabilised a brutal civil war, the culmination of a doctrine Blair had honed since Bosnia and Kosovo.

IRELAND: **Peace by Inches (1994–98)**

Ceasefires in 1994 began a stop-start march toward peace in Northern Ireland. Talks were fragile; bombs still exploded; hope repeatedly frayed. The breakthrough came with the Good Friday Agreement (10 April 1998) power-sharing, cross-border bodies, and a new framework for rights and policing.

Global Institutions and the "CNN Effect"

The 1990s were the decade of global architecture. The World Trade Organization (1995) replaced GATT; the International Criminal Tribunal for the former Yugoslavia (1993) broke new ground prosecuting war crimes and sexual violence; the Ottawa Treaty (1997) banned anti-personnel landmines. Satellite news created the "CNN effect," pulling distant crises onto British sofas and shaping political timetables.

Kate Adie and other correspondents reported from front lines; lawyers, medics, and logisticians carried NGO operations; academics and advocates reframed conflict through the lens of human rights and gender-based violence.

Globalisation and Everyday Life

While politicians wrestled with treaties and wars, globalisation transformed daily life:

Budget airlines like easyJet (founded in 1995) and Ryanair turned Europe into a weekend playground.

Fast-food chains spread across every high street, convenience and Americanisation in a cardboard wrapper.

Satellite TV brought CNN, MTV, Euronews, and a flood of niche channels; Sky moved from sport to news and entertainment, fragmenting the audience but widening horizons.

. . .

Aid, Activism, and "Ethical" Foreign Policy

The 1990s saw a surge in global activism: debt relief campaigns, fair-trade labels, anti-landmine lobbying. Princess Diana's walk through an Angolan minefield (January 1997) crystallised public attention and helped propel the Ottawa Treaty later that year.

After Labour's 1997 victory, Robin Cook promised an "ethical foreign policy"; DFID (the Department for International Development) was created with Clare Short as its first Secretary of State, signalling a new focus on poverty reduction and humanitarian response. NGOs like Oxfam, Save the Children, Amnesty, and a host of smaller outfits grew, offering new pathways into diplomacy, development, and international law.

The end of apartheid and the start of Nelson Mandela's presidency (1994) became a touchstone for what peaceful transition could look like, celebrated by British anti-apartheid campaigners who had sustained decades of solidarity, many of them women.

Why It Mattered

The 1990s left Britain torn between pride in its global role and doubt about its European future. Maastricht sowed seeds of Brexit by unleashing Conservative divisions that never healed. Black Wednesday scarred confidence in managed exchange rates and the euro project. Bosnia and Kosovo previewed the moral and legal dilemmas of humanitarian war that would define the 2000s.

Globalisation reshaped daily life: cheap travel democratised leisure; food and media diversified habits and tastes. Women gained workplace rights via EU law, took visible roles in activism and aid, and carried much of the service-sector burden.

The 1990s showed Britain straddling multiple worlds, European but uneasy, global but uncertain, proud of its past but unsure of its future. Those tensions would soon break the surface.

Mini Timeline – Europe and the World

1991 – Gulf War (Jan–Feb); Soviet Union collapses; end of the Cold War

1992 – Maastricht Treaty signed (7 Feb); UK Black Wednesday (16 Sep) exit from ERM

1992–95 – Bosnian War; Britain contributes to UN and NATO missions

1994 – Channel Tunnel opens; Rwanda genocide; IRA and loyalist ceasefires begin in Northern Ireland

1995 – World Trade Organization (WTO) founded; easyJet launched

1996 – EU bans British beef exports amid BSE crisis

1997 – Hong Kong handover (30 Jun); Diana's landmine campaign (Jan); Ottawa Treaty banning landmines (Dec); DFID created; "ethical foreign policy" announced

1998 – Good Friday Agreement (10 Apr)

1998–99 – Kosovo conflict; UK joins NATO bombing campaign

1999 – Euro launched (1 Jan) without UK participation; Seattle WTO protests highlight globalisation's critics

11. MEDIA REVOLUTION

The 1990s transformed how Britain consumed news, gossip, and entertainment. At the start of the decade, information came at fixed times: the Nine O'clock News, the morning papers, the Sunday colour supplements. By its end, Sky News was broadcasting 24/7, tabloids were setting political agendas, and celebrity magazines were creating stars from thin air. The media revolution didn't just change what people watched and read; it changed how Britain thought about privacy, power, and truth itself.

THE SKY REVOLUTION

Sky News had launched in 1989, but it came into its own in the 1990s. Suddenly, news was always happening. The Gulf War of 1991 became the first "television war," with missile strikes broadcast live into British living rooms. CNN pioneered the model globally, but Sky brought it home.

The psychological impact was profound. Major events such as Black Wednesday, IRA bombs, royal scandals no longer were a brief 'newsflash' and back to the main show and then waited for the evening bulletin. Rolling news created an appetite for instant reaction, immediate analysis, and constant updates that reshaped political communication.

For women in journalism, the expansion created new opportunities. Sky needed anchors and correspondents around the clock, opening doors for Kay Burley, Anna Botting, and Julie Etchingham. Yet the relentless pace also reinforced a macho newsroom culture of long hours and high pressure.

The murder of BBC presenter Jill Dando in 1999 showed how far the new media logic had gone. As the trusted face of *Crimewatch*, she was both a journalist and a celebrity. Her death shocked the nation, but it was also consumed as rolling coverage, with wall-to-wall speculation and surveillance footage turning tragedy into spectacle. Dando's case revealed the double edge of the 24-hour news cycle: nothing, not even the murder of one of its own, was exempt from its glare.

The Tabloid Kingmakers

If Sky provided the speed, the tabloids supplied the bite. The Sun, Daily Mail, Daily Mirror *and* News of the World reached peak circulation in the 1990s, with millions of daily readers and the power to make or break reputations.

The Sun's boast: "It's The Sun Wot Won It" after John Major's 1992 victory symbolised that influence. When the paper switched sides to back Tony Blair in 1997, it reflected a broader shift: New Labour understood that winning Murdoch mattered as much as winning marginals.

For women, tabloids were a double-edged sword. Female editors like Rebekah Wade (later Brooks) reached powerful positions, but the papers themselves continued to objectify women through Page 3, kiss-and-tell exposés, and relentless scrutiny of female celebrities' bodies and relationships.

Diana in particular, was both celebrated and hunted by the tabloid press, a tension that ended in tragedy.

THE BIRTH of Spin

The 1990s saw the professionalisation of political communication. Alastair Campbell, Blair's press secretary, pioneered rapid rebuttal, message discipline, and a ruthless focus on presentation. Peter Mandelson, dubbed "the Prince of Darkness," orchestrated New Labour's image with a precision no previous government had attempted.

The Conservatives struggled to keep up. John Major's press conferences became exercises in damage limitation, while Blair's team treated every photo op and soundbite as a strategic performance. Women like Anji Hunter, Blair's trusted aide, played crucial behind-the-scenes roles as gatekeepers and organisers, ensuring the machine ran smoothly.

Spin blurred the line between policy and performance. Journalists began covering the strategy behind announcements as much as the announcements themselves. Politics became theatre, with presentation often outweighing substance a shift that still defines British politics today.

MAGAZINES, Celebrity, and Heat

The 1990s saw an explosion of magazines. Glossy women's titles like Elle, Cosmopolitan, and Marie Claire expanded their reach, while lad mags like Loaded and FHM dominated male readerships. Both sold not just content but lifestyles, setting the tone of the culture.

In 1999, Heat reinvented celebrity journalism. Unlike tabloids, it invited readers into wardrobes and living rooms, turning fame into lifestyle content. It blurred gossip and aspiration, paving the way for the obsessive celebrity week-lies of the 2000s and, later, Instagram. For women, this was double-edged: female celebrities were more visible than ever but also scrutinised and mocked with unprecedented intensity.

Diana and the Media Mirror

No figure embodied the contradictions of the 1990s media more than Princess Diana. From her wedding in 1981 to her Panorama interview in 1995, she lived under constant scrutiny. But Diana also learned to use the media: cooper-ating with Andrew Morton's biography, inviting cameras to film her walking through minefields, and using television interviews to tell her own story.

Her death in 1997 while being pursued by paparazzi sparked a reckoning. Critics assailed the Press Complaints Commission, tabloids became temporarily chastened, and millions questioned whether the media itself was responsi-ble. Yet, demand for royal stories never diminished. Diana's relationship with the press was symbiotic: she needed them, they needed her, and in the end, both were consumed by the cycle.

Comedy and satire

The 1990s media also dismantled deference. Shows like Have I Got News for You (1990) and The Day Today (1994) lampooned politicians and broadcasters alike. Steve Coogan's Alan Partridge embodied the absurdity of media egos, while Caroline Aherne's The Royle Family (1998) turned the living room sofa into high culture.

Women were not only starring but writing and shaping tone. Aherne, Armando Iannucci's collaborators, and Jo

Brand all brought new perspectives to comedy. Satire blurred into reality, with politicians sometimes more worried about how they looked on TV than how they governed.

GLOBALISATION OF MEDIA

Britain wasn't just producing culture; it was consuming it. American imports like Friends, Frasier, and The Simpsons dominated British schedules, proof that globalisation flowed both ways. Coffee-shop culture, sitcom humour, and glossy US drama seeped into everyday life.

At the same time, British formats began their global journey. Who Wants to Be a Millionaire? (1998) became an international franchise. Changing Rooms pioneered makeover TV. The line between entertainment and lifestyle blurred, setting the stage for reality television's explosion in the 2000s.

Why It Mattered

The media revolution of the 1990s created the template for today's media culture. 24-hour news cycles, political spin, lad mags, Heat-style gossip, and Diana's symbiotic relationship with the press all reshaped how Britain consumed information.

For women, it was particularly complex. Female journalists and editors gained visibility and influence, while female celebrities dominated covers. Yet the same media system amplified objectification, scrutiny, and harassment.

Most of all, the 1990s ended deference. Politicians, royals, and institutions were no longer guaranteed respect. Media turned them into entertainment, reducing authority figures to characters in a national soap opera. The legacies, cynicism, spin, and the merging of news and spectacle, still shape Britain's public life today.

. . .

Mini Timeline – Media Revolution

- **1990** – *Have I Got News for You* launches.
- **1991** – Gulf War becomes first "24-hour war."
- **1992** – *Diana: Her True Story* serialised.
- **1994** – *The Day Today* parodies rolling news; *Loaded* peaks.
- **1995** – Diana's Panorama interview (22.8m viewers).
- **1997** – Diana's death sparks media ethics debate.
- **1998** – *FHM* circulation peaks; *Who Wants to Be a Millionaire?* launches.
- **1999** – *Heat* magazine launches; Jill Dando murdered; *The Royle Family* debuts.

12. MAGAZINES, CELEBRITY, AND DIANA

$\mathscr{\text{—}}$

$\mathcal{I}$f television provided the soundtrack of the 1990s, magazines were its glossy mirror. Week by week, issue by issue, they told the story of what mattered, or what was made to matter in British culture. Page 3 girls, Spice Girls, "ladettes," and royals shared the same newsstands, all consumed through the lens of an expanding celebrity culture. The press didn't just reflect fame; it manufactured it, commodified it, and, in some cases, destroyed it. At the centre of this media storm was one woman: Princess Diana.

DIANA: **The People's Princess**

No figure was more entangled in 1990s celebrity culture than Princess Diana. She had been a media phenomenon since her 1981 wedding to Prince Charles, but the 1990s turned her from royal consort into global icon.

Diana learned to use the press. She cooperated with Andrew Morton's 1992 book Diana: Her True Story, secretly recording tapes that revealed her unhappy marriage, struggles with bulimia, and suicide attempts. She embraced photo opportunities, from visiting AIDS patients to walking through minefields in Angola, crafting an image of compassion that captivated the world.

Her interview with Martin Bashir on Panorama in 1995 was watched by nearly 23 million viewers, was a cultural earthquake. Her declaration that "there were three of us in this marriage" not only shook the monarchy but showed that television could be used as a confessional pulpit.

Yet Diana also lived with the relentless intrusion of paparazzi lenses. Tabloids tracked her holidays, relationships, and even her sons. On 31 August 1997, chased by photographers in Paris, her car crashed, killing her and her companion Dodi Fayed. The reaction was unprecedented: seas of flowers outside Kensington Palace, mourning crowds in Hyde Park, and a funeral watched by an estimated 2.5 billion people worldwide.

For Britain, her death was more than a royal tragedy. It was a moment of national reckoning with the media. Had the press gone too far? Had tabloids and paparazzi killed the princess they adored? For weeks, headlines turned inward, criticising the very culture that had profited from her image.

Lad Mags and the Sexual Revolution Repackaged

The launch of Loaded magazine in 1994 reshaped British publishing. Marketed as cheeky and irreverent, it celebrated football, beer, and "birds" in equal measure. Its success spawned imitators like FHM and Maxim, which peaked at circulations of over 700,000 by the decade's end. They offered a laddish fantasy world, funny, blokey, aspirational, with scantily clad women as central props.

For men, lad mags seemed like harmless fun. For women, they were a mixed blessing: on one hand, they acknowledged female sexuality as mainstream; on the other, they objectified and trivialised women in print runs read by millions. Many feminists saw them as a backlash against the gains of the 1980s, packaging sexism as banter.

WOMEN'S MAGAZINES and Girl Power

If lad mags sold laddishness, women's magazines sold empowerment. Cosmopolitan told readers they could have careers, sex lives, and style. Just 17 and Sugar offered teenage girls advice on boys, fashion, and the minefield of growing up. Glossy monthlies like *Elle* and *Marie Claire* brought global fashion and feminist articles into British homes.

By the late 1990s, these magazines were colliding with the rise of Girl Power. The Spice Girls didn't just dominate the music charts, they dominated covers, with each interview or photo shoot offering readers lessons in identity, style, and confidence. For young women, this blend of pop and publishing was intoxicating.

HEAT and the Birth of Celebrity Gossip Culture

In 1999, Heat magazine redefined the genre. Instead of presenting celebrity as distant glamour, it made famous lives seem close-up, every day, even a little shabby. Paparazzi shots of celebrities buying groceries or walking down the street sat alongside fashion spreads and relationship speculation. It was the template for the gossip magazine boom of the 2000s and, eventually, the social media culture of the 2010s.

Women were both the stars and the audience of this new culture. Female celebrities were scrutinised and mocked for weight gain, fashion slips, or failed romances but women were also the editors, writers, and readers driving circulation. Fame had become a feedback loop: created, packaged, and consumed on a weekly cycle.

. . .

Women, Fame, and Double Standards

Diana's story was emblematic of a wider pattern. Female celebrities in the 1990s were celebrated, sold, and scrutinised with unprecedented intensity. Those in the public eye like Kate Winslet and Emma Thompson, models like Kate Moss, and pop stars from Geri Halliwell to Britney Spears were all made into icons and all judged ruthlessly for their bodies, romances, and choices.

Meanwhile, male celebrities were rarely treated with the same level of surveillance. The decade made women hyper-visible but often stripped them of agency. As Diana's life showed, fame in the 1990s could be as destructive as it was empowering.

Why It Mattered

The magazine and celebrity culture of the 1990s created the template for the world we now inhabit. Heat was the forerunner of social media gossip. Lad mags normalised "banter" as a cover for sexism. Women's glossies turned empowerment into a marketable product. Diana's life, and death, demonstrated the power of media to build and break icons.

For women, the contradictions were sharpest. They were editors and readers, pop stars and pin-ups, queens and cover girls. The media made them visible but rarely on their own terms. The 1990s taught Britain that fame was no longer reserved for the elite but also that fame could consume those who carried it.

Mini Timeline – Magazines, Celebrity, and Diana

- **1992** – Andrew Morton publishes *Diana: Her True Story*.
- **1994** – *Loaded* launches; lad mag era begins.
- **1995** – Diana's *Panorama* interview shocks Britain.
- **1996** – *FHM* circulation surpasses 750,000.
- **1997** – Diana dies in Paris car crash; unprecedented public mourning.
- **1998** – *Cosmopolitan* and *Elle* circulation peaks; women's glossies dominate.
- **1999** – *Heat* magazine launches, reinventing celebrity gossip.

13. COMEDY AND ENTERTAINMENT

If politics was spin and music was swagger, the 1990s also belonged to comedy. British humour reinvented itself in the decade, moving from the blokey banter of Men Behaving Badly to the surreal wit of The Fast Show, the cringe of Alan Partridge, and the quiet brilliance of The Royle Family. Comedy and entertainment didn't just make people laugh; they redefined what Britishness looked and sounded like.

MEN BEHAVING BADLY and Lad Culture on Screen

In the early 1990s, Men Behaving Badly captured the spirit of lad culture. Martin Clunes and Neil Morrissey played housemates obsessed with lager, football, and dodging responsibility. It was cheeky, laddish, and hugely popular, running for six series.

The show chimed with the era of Loaded and FHM, but it also sparked criticism for normalising immaturity and sexism. Women in the series were long-suffering girlfriends or the punchline. For feminists, it epitomised the limits of the decade's humour: funny, yes, but at whose expense?

The Fast Show and Catchphrase Britain

By the mid-1990s, British comedy shifted towards sketch shows. The Fast Show (1994–97) reinvented the form with rapid-fire sketches and catchphrases that slipped into everyday conversation: "Suits you, sir!", "Scorchio!", "This week I have been mostly eating..."

The show reflected a Britain comfortable with surrealism and satire, poking fun at stereotypes from weather forecasters to fashionistas. Importantly, it featured strong female performers like Arabella Weir, whose "Does my bum look big in this?" sketch became iconic, capturing the anxieties of 1990s body culture.

Alan Partridge and Media Satire

If The Fast Show gave Britain catchphrases, Alan Partridge gave it awkwardness. Created by Steve Coogan, Partridge began on The Day Today before starring in Knowing Me, Knowing You and later I'm Alan Partridge (1997).

Partridge was a grotesque but oddly sympathetic caricature of the media age: desperate for fame, blind to his flaws, always one gaffe away from disaster. He satirised not just television egos but Britain's obsession with minor celebrity. The character proved so enduring that he remains part of Britain's comedy DNA decades later.

The Royle Family: Comedy in a Living Room

In 1998, Caroline Aherne transformed British television with The Royle Family. Eschewing laugh tracks and punchlines, it placed a working-class Manchester family on a sofa, watching television. Nothing much happened, and that was the point.

It was revolutionary: the comedy came from everyday life and affection, rather than jokes. Aherne, as co-creator, writer, and performer, brought a female voice and authenticity rarely seen in sitcoms. The Royles represented Britain as it really was, messy, mundane, and deeply human.

GAME SHOWS and Reality Experiments

Beyond sitcoms, entertainment formats evolved. Who Wants to Be a Millionaire? (1998) turned quiz shows into high drama, with Chris Tarrant's "final answer" catchphrase echoing across living rooms. Lottery shows, fronted by Dale Winton and Carol Vorderman, mixed chance with entertainment.

Reality television also began to stir. Changing Rooms (1996) pioneered makeover TV, while Big Brother launched in the Netherlands in 1999 and was about to land in Britain. The idea of ordinary people becoming stars was brewing a cultural shift that would explode in the 2000s.

AMERICAN IMPORTS and Global Humour

Alongside homegrown comedy, American shows found loyal audiences. Friends became Friday night ritual, shaping speech, fashion, and coffee culture. The Simpsons brought sharp, satirical family comedy that resonated with both children and adults. Frasier offered a more sophisticated wit, while South Park arrived at the decade's end to scandalise parents and delight teenagers.

British comedy was globalising. Audiences switched

easily between Manchester sofas and Manhattan lofts, between Alan Partridge's radio booth and Homer Simpson's Springfield sofa. Entertainment was becoming borderless.

WOMEN IN COMEDY

The 1990s finally saw women's voices gain ground in comedy. Caroline Aherne was the most celebrated, but Jo Brand built a career on acerbic stand-up, turning domestic frustrations into sharp political commentary. Jennifer Saunders and Dawn French continued their partnership with Absolutely Fabulous (1992 onwards) skewering fashion, PR, and celebrity culture through the chaos of Edina and Patsy.

These shows gave women comic agency, not as foils or punchlines, but as creators and stars. Yet the industry remained male-dominated, with far fewer women writing or headlining shows than men. The female-led successes of the 1990s laid the groundwork that later generations would build on.

WHY IT MATTERED

Comedy and entertainment in the 1990s captured the contradictions of the decade. Lad culture's blokey humour coexisted with Caroline Aherne's subtlety. Alan Partridge mocked celebrity while Heat celebrated it. The Royles sat on their sofa while Friends drank coffee in Central Perk.

For women, the 1990s brought breakthroughs and barriers. They were visible in sitcoms and sketch shows but rarely dominated writers' rooms or production companies. Yet the voices of Aherne, Brand, French, and Saunders proved that women's comedy could define the national mood.

The legacy of 1990s entertainment is still felt today. Catchphrases, cringe comedy, makeover shows, and reality

TV all trace their roots back to the decade. More than just laughs, 1990s comedy showed Britain to be messy, contradictory, and endlessly funny.

MINI TIMELINE – Comedy and Entertainment

- **1990** – *Have I Got News for You* launches.
- **1992** – *Absolutely Fabulous* debuts.
- **1994** – *The Fast Show* begins; *Friends* arrives in the UK.
- **1995** – *Men Behaving Badly* peaks in popularity.
- **1997** – *I'm Alan Partridge* airs; satire of media culture.
- **1998** – *The Royle Family* debuts; *Who Wants to Be a Millionaire?* launches.
- **1999** – *South Park* reaches UK screens; *Big Brother* launches in the Netherlands.

14. GROWING UP IN THE 1990S

or young people, the 1990s were both liberating and pressured. This was the first decade when teenagers felt part of a global youth culture, listening to the same CDs, playing the same computer games, and watching the same TV as their peers abroad. Yet it was also a time when education became increasingly competitive, childhood increasingly commercialised, and young people found themselves at the centre of public debates about morality and the future.

Childhood was no longer considered a private, protected stage of life. Politicians, the press, and parents alike dissected how children played, what they wore, and what they consumed. At the same time, young people themselves gained new visibility on MTV, in fashion, in magazines, and on the high street. The contradictions of the decade were stark: celebration of youth as culture-makers alongside suspicion of youth as troublemakers.

CLASSROOMS AND CURRICULUM

The National Curriculum, introduced in 1988, defined the 1990s classroom. Every child in England and Wales was now taught the same core subjects, tested through Standard Assessment Tests (SATs) at ages 7, 11, and 14. Parents scrutinised results; children carried the burden of national comparison. League tables, introduced in 1992, ranked schools publicly, creating winners and losers in full view.

Ofsted, founded the same year, introduced rigorous inspections that could make or break reputations. The stress filtered down: teachers spoke of "teaching to the test," while parents fretted over which catchment area could secure their child the "right" school.

John Major's "Back to Basics" campaign in 1993, which called for a return to traditional values, was often interpreted as a demand for stricter schools and disciplined youth. Yet, the same years saw rising class sizes, underfunding, and teacher strikes. Debates about grammar schools versus comprehensives resurfaced, fuelling divisions about what education was for: social mobility, discipline, or creativity.

CHILDHOOD, Play, and Pop Culture

For children, the 1990s were an age of toys, TV, and fast-changing fads. Tamagotchis, Furbies, Pokémon cards, and Beanie Babies created playground economies where value shifted overnight. Panini football stickers, Pogs, and yo-yos came and went in crazes that seemed to unite every playground in Britain.

Children's television shaped daily rhythms: Blue Peter soldiered on with sticky-back plastic, but new formats emerged. Byker Grove (starring Ant & Dec) and Grange Hill tackled serious issues like drugs and bullying. SM:TV Live (from 1998) mixed comedy and pop performance, while Teletubbies (1997) became a global toddler phenomenon.

Books continued to matter. Goosebumps series (R.L. Stine) thrilled children, while Jacqueline Wilson's novels gave many girls their first experience of fiction that reflected their real lives; divorce, friendship troubles, and working-class families. Then, in 1997, Harry Potter and the Philosopher's Stone appeared, sparking a cultural revolution in reading.

Magazines fuelled teenage identity. Just 17 and Sugar mixed dating advice with fashion tips, diets, and boyband posters. Smash Hits, still thriving, taught fans lyrics before the internet could. Yet alongside fun came pressure: narrow ideals of beauty, diets marketed to teenagers, and articles about sex and relationships delivered in tones half-scandalised, half-instructive.

Moral Panics and Young People

The 1990s made young people objects of anxiety. The murder of James Bulger in 1993 by two ten-year-old boys became a national trauma. The press questioned whether childhood innocence was dead, while politicians debated lowering the age of criminal responsibility. The case reinforced fears of a "feral youth," and Denise Fergus, James's mother, became an enduring campaigner for victims' rights.

The Criminal Justice Act 1994 extended these anxieties into youth leisure. By criminalising gatherings with "repetitive beats," it explicitly targeted rave culture, casting young people as threats to public order. "Hoodies," "joyriders," and "teen mums" became tabloid shorthand for social decline.

Women were especially scrutinised. The rise of the "ladette" - drinking, smoking, and swearing like their male peers, was alternately celebrated as feminist rebellion and condemned as vulgarity. Teenage pregnancy, which peaked in the mid-1990s, was treated as a national scandal, despite complex causes. Girls bore the brunt of being cultural battle-grounds for morality.

HIGHER EDUCATION and Student Life

Universities expanded rapidly. In 1992, former polytechnics became universities, broadening access and changing perceptions of higher education. Participation rates doubled across the decade: a profound social shift. But expansion came with new costs.

In 1998, Labour introduced tuition fees (£1,000 per year), ending the tradition of free higher education. Student loans, introduced in 1990, expanded in scope. Many students entered adulthood in debt for the first time in British history. Protests erupted: the National Union of Students organised marches, while grassroots activists staged sit-ins and occupations.

Campus life reflected broader culture. Student unions hosted Britpop gigs, comedy nights, and debates. Student politics fought over tuition fees, fair trade coffee, and anti-racism campaigns. Women gained greater visibility in leadership, though gender divides persisted in academic subjects: men dominated engineering and technology, while women clustered in humanities, education, and nursing.

YOUTH AND TECHNOLOGY

The decade saw teenagers among the earliest adopters of new technology. Home PCs appeared in classrooms and bedrooms: Acorn Archimedes in schools, beige Windows 95 desktops at home. Typing pools gave way to pupils writing essays in Word.

By the late 90s, the internet reached teenagers via dial-up. Chatrooms, MSN Messenger (launched 1999), and forums created new forms of interaction, often anonymous, sometimes risky, and almost always exciting. For isolated young people, especially LGBTQ+ teens silenced by Section 28, these online spaces offered rare solidarity.

Gaming was equally transformative. PlayStation (1995), Nintendo 64 (1997), and Game Boy put interactive entertainment in bedrooms and pockets. Games like Tomb Raider, GoldenEye 007, and Pokémon Red/Blue created shared experiences across schools and neighbourhoods. For girls, Lara Croft was both problematic and empowering: a hyper-sexualised heroine, but also the first time many girls saw themselves at the centre of adventure.

Gap Years and Global Horizons

The 1990s saw the birth of the gap year boom. Once the preserve of the privileged, falling airfares opened it to the middle classes. With easyJet (1995) and Ryanair's no-frills model (1995–96), students could afford city breaks and backpacking trips. Interrailing across Europe became a rite of passage; Lonely Planet guides shaped journeys through Asia, Australia, and South America.

For young women, this was liberation and risk. Independence abroad offered new freedom but also provoked warnings about safety and propriety. The gap year debate mirrored broader anxieties: was youth travel broadening horizons or indulging privilege? Either way, it reflected a Britain more globally connected than ever before.

· · ·

Why It Mattered

The 1990s reshaped what it meant to be young in Britain. Education became standardised, measured, and politicised. Childhood became commercialised through toys, magazines, and media, while teenagers became scapegoats for moral decline. University access widened but was redefined by debt.

For women and girls, the stakes were high. They were expected to excel academically while navigating a media culture obsessed with their looks and behaviour. They consumed new technologies and helped define youth culture, yet their freedom was frequently policed.

Youth in the 1990s were globalised, mediated, and scrutinised as never before. They were the first to come of age with email, PlayStations, and Harry Potter. They were also the first to be told they would pay for their education and live under the shadow of constant comparison. The decade didn't just change youth it made youth the central lens through which Britain debated its future.

Mini Timeline – Youth and Education

1991 – SATs introduced in primary schools

1992 – Ofsted founded; former polytechnics gain university status

1993 – James Bulger murdered; youth crime panic dominates headlines

1994 – Criminal Justice Act targets raves and "repetitive beats"

1995 – easyJet founded; gap year and budget travel culture expands

1997 – Harry Potter and the Philosopher's Stone published

1998 – Labour introduces tuition fees; NUS protests erupt

1999 – MSN Messenger launches; internet becomes part of teenage life

15. FASHION AND STYLE

❧

*F*rom Grunge to Glitter
        The 1990s were a decade of contradictions in fashion. On one hand, designers and magazines pushed high-concept glamour; on the other, teenagers in Doc Martens and oversized hoodies declared their own rebellion. Style became more eclectic than ever before: grunge flannel shirts, Britpop parkas, Spice Girls platforms, minimalist slip dresses, and "heroin chic" all jostled for attention.

Fashion wasn't just fabric; it was identity. Youth claimed subcultures through what they wore. Women, in particular, navigated competing expectations: be sexy, be strong, be skinny, be sporty, be yourself. In a decade defined by consumerism and celebrity, clothing was both armour and performance.

GRUNGE AND STREETWEAR

Imported from Seattle, grunge landed in Britain in the early 1990s. Nirvana and Pearl Jam inspired a wave of plaid shirts, ripped jeans, and Converse trainers. The look rejected

1980s glamour in favour of deliberate scruffiness. For teenagers, it was an affordable rebellion and charity shops suddenly became style meccas.

Grunge also blurred gender lines. Women in oversized jumpers and combat boots rejected the body-conscious silhouettes of the 80s. Yet even as it celebrated messiness, the fashion industry commodified it, with Kate Moss styled in "heroin chic" shoots that glamorised exhaustion and thinness.

Streetwear also boomed. Labels like Adidas, Reebok, and Nike became everyday uniform, especially with the rise of rave and hip-hop culture. Tracksuits, baseball caps, and trainers migrated from sports fields to high streets. This crossover blurred class markers: expensive designer trainers became symbols of status as much as practicality.

BRITPOP CHIC

Britpop didn't just soundtrack the decade, it dressed it. Bands like Oasis and Blur inspired their followers with mod revival looks, Harrington jackets, and Fred Perry polos. The parka became iconic thanks to Liam Gallagher.

Women were equally part of the scene. Justine Frischmann of Elastica embodied art-school cool: sharp haircuts, leather jackets, and an anti-glamour sensibility. Sleeper's Louise Wener presented an alternative to the Spice Girls, using fashion as subtle rebellion rather than spectacle.

The look was defiantly British, rooted in 1960s nostalgia but updated for the 1990s. Union Jack motifs, most famously Geri Halliwell's 1997 Brit Awards dress, transformed national symbols into fashion statements.

GIRL POWER on the Catwalk

No one embodied 1990s fashion more than the Spice Girls. Each member's look was instantly recognisable: Sporty in tracksuits, Scary in animal prints, Baby in pastels, Posh in sleek black dresses, Ginger in Union Jack minidress and platforms. Their branding turned clothing into identity, and identity into power.

High heels gave way to Buffalo platform trainers, copied by teenage girls worldwide. Suddenly, individuality was fashionable. Young women were told they could be sporty, posh, or babyish. The Spice Girls democratised fashion: their outfits were as likely to be found in high street shops as designer boutiques.

Supermodels and "Heroin Chic"

The supermodel era continued into the 1990s with Naomi Campbell, Kate Moss, Linda Evangelista, and Christy Turlington dominating catwalks and covers. Campbell, a Black British model, broke barriers by fronting major campaigns, though she also spoke candidly about racism in the industry.

Kate Moss became the most controversial figure. Discovered in 1988, by the mid-1990s she embodied "heroin chic": pale skin, thin frame, dishevelled glamour. Her Calvin Klein campaigns sparked fierce debates about fashion's promotion of unhealthy body ideals. Critics argued the look romanticised addiction and eating disorders; defenders said it reflected the raw edge of youth culture.

Designers and Avant-Garde Britain

British designers defined global style. Alexander McQueen, dubbed the "enfant terrible" of fashion, staged dramatic runway shows, models in cages, spray-painted live on stage, that blurred art and fashion. His designs combined gothic imagination with impeccable tailoring, shocking and inspiring in equal measure.

Stella McCartney, daughter of Paul McCartney, launched her career in the 1990s with collections that mixed accessibility and chic. Known for her ethical approach, she represented a generational shift in fashion's values.

Vivienne Westwood carried her punk legacy into the decade, fusing political provocation with haute couture. Her influence on both streetwear and high fashion ensured that rebellion remained part of Britain's fashion DNA.

Minimalism and the High Street

Not everyone wanted grunge or glitter. Minimalism, epitomised by Calvin Klein and Jil Sander, offered slip dresses, monochrome palettes, and understated chic. For working women, this look carried professional authority without the power suits of the 1980s.

At the same time, the British high street exploded. Topshop, New Look, River Island, and Miss Selfridge churned out fast-fashion imitations of catwalk trends at affordable prices. H&M opened its first UK store in 1998, signalling a new wave of globalised retail.

Teenagers and young women became the high street's target market. Disposable fashion encouraged weekly shopping trips, loyalty cards, and constant reinvention. The high street wasn't just commerce; it was a social space where youth performed identity.

Body Image and Fitness Culture

Fashion and body image were inseparable. The obsession with thinness reached new extremes. Kate Moss's infamous phrase "nothing tastes as good as skinny feels" (though disputed) became shorthand for a culture where diets and eating disorders loomed large.

Magazines like Cosmopolitan and Elle mixed fashion spreads with diet tips and celebrity workout routines. Fitness culture grew alongside: gyms like David Lloyd expanded, aerobics videos from celebrities like Cindy Crawford and Mr Motivator became staples in living rooms.

The contradictions were glaring. Women were told to be thin yet curvy, natural yet glamorous, powerful yet pleasing. Fashion both empowered and constrained, offering self-expression but also relentless pressure.

SUBCULTURES AND IDENTITY

Beyond mainstream fashion, subcultures thrived. Goths embraced black velvet and eyeliner; ravers wore neon, whistles, and glow sticks; skaters adopted baggy jeans and Vans. Youth claimed identity through clothing that marked them as insiders or outsiders.

Multicultural Britain reshaped fashion, too. Bhangra club nights inspired fusion outfits; Afro-Caribbean styles like braids and bold prints gained visibility in mainstream culture. Mehndi (henna) became a temporary fashion craze among white teenagers, while also sparking debates about cultural appropriation.

WHY IT MATTERED

Fashion in the 1990s was more than clothing; it was a battleground for identity. Grunge rejected glamour, Britpop reclaimed Britishness, the Spice Girls democratised style, and supermodels embodied contradictions of beauty and pressure.

For women, the stakes were especially high. They were both celebrated as trendsetters and scrutinised as objects. They drove consumer markets yet faced relentless body policing. The industry opened doors for diversity; Naomi Campbell on the catwalk, Stella McCartney designing ethically but change was uneven and slow.

Fashion in the 1990s captured the contradictions of the decade itself: rebellious yet commercial, liberating yet pressurised, global yet intensely personal. What people wore in the 1990s didn't just follow trends, it defined how they saw themselves in a rapidly changing Britain.

MINI TIMELINE – **Fashion and Style**

1990 – Naomi Campbell becomes first Black model on cover of British Vogue's September issue

1992 – Absolutely Fabulous debuts, parodying fashion and consumerism

1993 – Kate Moss rises to prominence; "heroin chic" enters debate

1994 – Church of England allows women priests; Vicar of Dibley reflects new female authority in pop culture and fashion

1996 – Geri Halliwell's Union Jack dress at Brit Awards becomes defining 90s image

1997 – Stella McCartney graduates Central Saint Martins; launches career

1998 – H&M opens first UK store; fast fashion globalises

1999 – Alexander McQueen named British Designer of the Year; his avant-garde shows redefine catwalks

16. WORK AND THE WORKPLACE

*F*rom Offices to Open Plan

The 1990s transformed how Britons worked. Offices moved from typewriters and filing cabinets to computers and email. Open-plan layouts replaced partitioned cubicles, reflecting new ideals of efficiency and transparency but often increasing noise and stress. Call centres proliferated, turning voices into labour. At the same time, "flexibility" became the buzzword of the age, promising freedom but often delivering insecurity.

Work was no longer just about wages; it was about identity, culture, and lifestyle. For women, the decade marked both opportunity and frustration: more entered the workforce than ever before, but the glass ceiling remained firmly in place.

Email, PCs, and the Digital Desk

The arrival of the personal computer changed the daily rhythm of work. By the mid-1990s, Windows 95 and Microsoft Office were standard across offices. Email began to replace memos, speeding communication but extending working hours into evenings and weekends.

Secretarial typing pools disappeared, replaced by Word and Excel on every desk. This shift cut some traditional jobs but expanded women's roles in administration, project management, and design. Yet IT departments and leadership in tech remained male-dominated.

By the decade's end, internet connections entered offices. Dial-up access and clunky web browsers promised efficiency but often delivered distraction. The dot-com bubble made "tech" glamorous, but for many employees the digital dawn meant endless training sessions and frustration with frozen screens.

CALL CENTRES and Service Work

One of the most visible symbols of 1990s work was the call centre. Cheap telecommunications and deregulated labour markets meant thousands of new jobs in phone-based customer service, from banks to utilities to catalogue orders.

For many women, call centres were both opportunity and trap. They offered flexible hours, part-time contracts, and accessible entry-level jobs, but also long shifts, low wages, and constant monitoring. Headsets and scripts symbolised both modern efficiency and a new form of workplace control.

The spread of call centres reflected the broader service economy. Manufacturing continued to decline, while retail, hospitality, and customer service expanded.

CASUAL FRIDAYS and Corporate Culture

Workplaces began to experiment with "casualisation." Casual Fridays, imported from the US, allowed employees to wear jeans and jumpers at the end of the week. For some, it was liberation from suits; for others, a confusing blurring of identities. What counted as "too casual"? Could women dress down without being judged as unprofessional?

Team-building weekends, away-days, and motivational posters became part of corporate culture. The language of management shifted too: buzzwords like "downsizing," "synergy," and "empowerment" entered office conversations. Satire thrived in this environment: The Office, though airing in 2001, grew directly out of 1990s workplace clichés.

WOMEN AT WORK

By 1997, 68% of women of working age were in employment, the highest ever recorded. Dual-income households became the norm, but childcare provision lagged. The National Childcare Strategy, launched in 1998, aimed to provide accessible, affordable, and quality childcare, with goals to reduce child poverty and support parents into work, but balancing work and family remained one of the decade's biggest challenges.

The gender pay gap persisted: women earned around 17% less than men for full-time work. Senior roles remained overwhelmingly male, with only a handful of female FTSE 100 directors by the end of the decade. Campaigns for equal pay, maternity rights, and workplace harassment policies gained momentum, often led by trade unions and grassroots women's groups.

At the same time, women were increasingly visible in professions once dominated by men: law, medicine, finance, and politics. Female solicitors and doctors entered in record numbers. Yet representation didn't always mean equality, progress in numbers often outpaced progress in power.

. . .

Zero-Hours and "Flexibility"

The word "flexibility" became the mantra of 1990s employment policy. Employers celebrated the ability to hire workers on temporary or zero-hours contracts, claiming it provided opportunity and adaptability. For many workers, it meant instability: shifts cancelled at short notice, no guaranteed income, and few employment rights.

Agency work and temping boomed, with companies like Manpower and Office Angels placing thousands in short-term roles. Some enjoyed the variety; others felt trapped in endless cycles of insecurity. The new economy rewarded adaptability but offered little loyalty.

Strikes, Pensions, and Union Decline

Trade unions, weakened by defeats in the 1980s, struggled in the 1990s. Membership continued to fall, from 13 million in 1979 to around 7 million by the mid-90s. Yet strikes still occurred: over pay, working conditions, and privatisations.

Public sector workers, nurses, teachers, transport staff, fought cuts and workload pressures by instigating industrial disputes. Yet media coverage often framed strikes as selfish or disruptive, reinforcing divisions between workers and the wider public.

Pensions became a growing concern. The shift from final-salary schemes to defined-contribution plans reduced security for future retirees. For women, who often had interrupted careers and lower earnings, the implications were particularly stark.

Diversity and Discrimination

The 1990s brought new conversations about diversity in

the workplace. The Disability Discrimination Act (1995) required reasonable adjustments for disabled employees. The Race Relations (Amendment) Act (2000) was still to come, but the Stephen Lawrence case (1993) had already forced employers to consider institutional racism.

Women of colour often faced double barriers, overlooked for promotion and concentrated in the lowest-paid jobs. LGBTQ+ employees still had little legal protection, with Section 28 contributing to a climate of silence. Yet grassroots workplace networks began forming, laying the groundwork for more inclusive policies in the 2000s.

THE WORK-LIFE DEBATE

By the late 1990s, the phrase "work-life balance" had entered everyday language. Longer hours in professional jobs collided with childcare, commuting, and exhaustion. Mobile phones and laptops began eroding the boundaries between the office and the home.

Some companies experimented with family-friendly policies, flexitime, or job-sharing, but progress was uneven. For many women, the promise of "having it all" felt like "doing it all," juggling career, childcare, and domestic responsibilities with little structural support.

WHY IT MATTERED

The 1990s reshaped Britain's working life. Technology revolutionised offices, call centres expanded, and service jobs replaced manufacturing. Corporate culture embraced buzzwords and casual Fridays, while insecurity grew through temping and zero-hours contracts.

For women, the changes were double-edged. More entered the workforce than ever before, and some rose into new professions. Yet pay gaps, childcare shortages, and precarious contracts meant progress was partial and fragile.

The decade showed that work was no longer just about a pay packet. It was about identity, culture, and the constant negotiation between freedom and insecurity. The 1990s workplace laid the foundations for today's gig economy, digital offices, and debates about balance. In both its promises and pressures, it shaped how Britain still works today.

Mini Timeline – Work and the Workplace

1990 – Student loans introduced; beginning of debt-funded education

1992 – League tables and Ofsted reshape schools; workplace targets rise

1995 – Disability Discrimination Act passed

1996 – "Casual Fridays" popularised in UK workplaces

1997 – Women's employment reaches 68% of working-age population

1998 – National Childcare Strategy launched

1999 – Zero-hours contracts become widespread in service industries

17. RELIGION AND BELIEF

*D*ecline and Continuity
    The 1990s were the decade when religion in Britain seemed to fade, yet it never disappeared. Weekly church attendance fell to below 10% by the decade's end, down from more than 50% in the 1950s. For many, Sunday mornings now meant shopping trips or football practice rather than pews and hymnbooks. The Church of England, long central to national identity, looked increasingly out of step with daily life.

Decline did not mean irrelevance. Cathedrals became important civic spaces, their soaring architecture hosting concerts, exhibitions, and national rituals. When Princess Diana died in 1997, Westminster Abbey became the focus of global mourning, proving that the old institutions could still carry meaning even in an increasingly secular society.

WOMEN in the Church

One of the most significant religious milestones of the century came in 1994, when the Church of England ordained women priests for the first time. Over 1,500 women were ordained in the first wave, many of them entering ministry after years of lay service. For congregations, the sight of a woman in a clerical collar was inspiring and controversial.

Debates raged in parishes, synods, and the press. Traditionalists threatened to leave the Church, while supporters hailed a new era of inclusivity. Women priests themselves often faced suspicion, patronising comments, and structural barriers. Yet their presence changed the face of Anglican worship and set a precedent that would eventually lead to women bishops in the 21st century.

In popular culture, this shift was captured by The Vicar of Dibley (1994), a sitcom starring Dawn French as a humorous, relatable female vicar. Fiction reflected fact: women clergy were no longer unthinkable; they were part of the British landscape.

FAITH AND POLITICS

Though formal churchgoing declined, religious language still coloured politics. John Major's "Back to Basics" campaign in 1993 appealed to traditional moral values, though it quickly collapsed under a wave of Tory scandals. Tony Blair, whose Catholicism remained understated in office, later admitted that his advisers often told him, "We don't do God." The caution reflected Britain's discomfort with overt religiosity in politics, contrasting with the United States.

Yet European integration meant religion entered politics indirectly. EU directives on maternity leave, equal pay, and working hours often intersected with moral debates about family life. At the same time, Britain's increasingly diverse faith communities began to organise politically, pressing for recognition and representation in local councils and national debates.

MULTIFAITH BRITAIN

The 1990s were years of visible religious plurality. Mosques, temples, gurdwaras, and Black-majority churches flourished in British cities, serving immigrant and second-generation communities. Faith schools expanded, sparking debates about multiculturalism and social cohesion.

Food, fashion, and festivals carried faith into mainstream life. Halal butchers, Diwali celebrations, Ramadan fasting, and Sikh Vaisakhi parades became increasingly familiar across towns and cities. For many immigrant families, religious institutions offered not just worship but community support, social services, and cultural continuity.

Women were often at the heart of these communities: organising events, teaching language and scripture classes, running charities, and navigating the negotiation between traditional expectations and modern Britain. Their visibility, particularly in Islamic dress, made them frequent subjects of political and media debates about integration and identity.

ISLAMOPHOBIA AND MEDIA Suspicion

While Britain became more multifaith, suspicion and hostility grew too. The Gulf War (1991) brought Muslim communities under sharper scrutiny. Asylum debates and fears about extremism in the mid-90s hardened attitudes further. Tabloid newspapers frequently portrayed Muslims as alien or threatening, laying the groundwork for Islamophobia that would intensify after 9/11.

Women in hijab often bore the brunt of this climate. Visible in workplaces, schools, and public life, they were sometimes celebrated as symbols of multicultural Britain but just as often stigmatised. The politics of clothing turned personal choices into public debates, forcing women into the role of cultural battlegrounds.

New Age and Alternative Beliefs

Alongside traditional religion and multicultural faith, the 1990s witnessed a boom in New Age spirituality. Astrology columns thrived in magazines, crystals and incense filled shops, and yoga and meditation classes entered leisure centres and gyms. Bookshops devoted whole sections to "mind-body-spirit," selling titles on self-help, Wicca, and alternative healing.

For many, New Age practices offered empowerment and community outside patriarchal religious structures. Pagan and Wiccan groups grew steadily, emphasising nature, female leadership, and alternative rituals.

The popularity of alternative spirituality reflected broader shifts: scepticism about institutions, desire for personal empowerment, and a search for meaning in an era of rapid change.

Rituals of Mourning and Belief

Even as formal religiosity declined, new rituals of belief and mourning emerged. Diana's death in 1997 triggered an extraordinary outpouring of grief. Millions left flowers, candles, and handwritten notes outside palaces and cathedrals. These acts, though secular, carried spiritual weight: they showed that ritual and collective mourning remained essential to British life.

Public vigils for tragedies such as Dunblane (1996) or Omagh (1998) also reflected this shift. Candles, flowers, and moments of silence became modern liturgies, blending religious traditions with civic solidarity.

Why It Mattered

Religion in the 1990s was not vanishing; it was transforming. Churches emptied, but women priests filled pulpits. Mosques and temples expanded, reflecting Britain's new diversity. Alternative spirituality flourished in shops and community halls. Public grief found expression in flowers and vigils rather than pews.

For women, the changes were profound. They gained long-denied authority in the Church of England, led community life in immigrant congregations, and drove participation in New Age movements. Yet they also bore the burdens of prejudice, whether as hijab-wearing professionals facing discrimination or as clergy navigating entrenched patriarchy.

The decade showed that belief in Britain was no longer about a single national church. It was about plurality, experimentation, and reinvention. Faith was less about Sunday sermons and more about identity, ritual, and resilience in a rapidly changing society.

Mini Timeline – **Religion and Belief**

1991 – Gulf War increases media focus on British Muslim communities

1992 – John Major launches "Back to Basics," appealing to moral values

1994 – Church of England ordains women priests for the first time

1995 – Mind-body-spirit publishing boom reflects New Age popularity

1996 – Dunblane massacre prompts candlelit vigils nationwide

1997 – Princess Diana's funeral at Westminster Abbey becomes global spiritual event

1998 – Debates intensify over faith schools and social cohesion

1999 – Pagan Federation formally recognised as a religious group in Britain

18. CRIME AND JUSTICE

Fear and Reality

The 1990s were marked by a deep tension between crime statistics and public perception. Crime rates peaked in the early part of the decade, with burglary, car theft, and violent offences all rising. By the late 1990s, recorded crime was falling, but fear remained high, fuelled by tabloid headlines and television images of youth violence, drugs, and "Broken Britain."

Women, long disproportionately the victims of domestic violence and sexual assault, saw their experiences addressed more visibly in public debate during this decade. They were also the moral authorities in campaigns for justice, and increasingly the professionals shaping law and policing. The decade was not just about criminal statistics, it was about who defined crime, who suffered from it, and who fought to change the system.

THE BULGER CASE and Its Aftermath

The abduction and murder of two-year-old James Bulger

by two ten-year-old boys in 1993 shocked the nation. While this case is remembered as one of the decade's darkest tragedies, its legacy in justice was equally profound. It sparked fierce debates about the age of criminal responsibility, the role of parents, and whether the justice system should punish or rehabilitate children.

The trial of the two boys, tried in an adult court, became a lightning rod for public anger and tabloid outrage. Campaigners like Denise Fergus, James's mother, gave voice to victims' rights in a way that reshaped legal discourse. The case became shorthand for the anxieties of the 1990s: fears about childhood innocence lost, about crime invading everyday spaces like shopping centres, and about whether Britain's justice system could cope with a changing society.

Policing in Transition

The police were under intense scrutiny in the 1990s. The Stephen Lawrence case (1993) and the subsequent Macpherson Report (1999) exposed "institutional racism" in the Metropolitan Police, forcing unprecedented reflection on discriminatory practices. Stop-and-search powers, community policing, and relations with minority communities all came under debate.

Women's roles in policing also expanded. By the end of the decade, women officers made up around 15% of the force, a steady rise from earlier generations. Yet sexism remained rife, with female officers often taking up many of the roles in "family liaison" or "domestic violence" rather than frontline leadership. The 1990s showed progress in numbers but also revealed how far the institution still had to go.

. . .

DNA and the Science of Justice

Britain was at the cutting edge of forensic science. Following the pioneering work of Sir Alec Jeffreys in the 1980s, the UK became the first country in the world to establish a national DNA database in 1995. By storing genetic profiles of offenders, police could match crime scene evidence with unprecedented accuracy.

The power of DNA transformed policing, solving cold cases and exonerating the wrongly convicted. Yet it also sparked civil liberties concerns: whose DNA was stored, how it was used, and whether innocent people's data could be kept indefinitely. For women, DNA offered hope of greater justice in rape cases, which had long suffered from low conviction rates. But systemic biases in the police and courts meant scientific tools alone could not erase entrenched inequalities.

Prisons, Privatisation, and Overcrowding

The 1990 Strangeways prison riot in Manchester, though beginning just before the decade, set the tone for debates about prison conditions in the 1990s. Overcrowding, violence, and poor conditions were not new, but they became constant themes of political debate. By the mid-90s, the prison population surged past 60,000, fuelled by tougher sentencing and "tough on crime" rhetoric.

For the first time, private prisons opened in Britain, beginning with HMP Wolds in 1992. Critics warned of profit-driven justice; supporters argued they could be more efficient. In practice, privatisation created a patchwork of standards and accountability that persists to this day.

Women in prison remained a largely hidden issue. Rising numbers were incarcerated for non-violent offences, often linked to poverty, drugs, or petty crime. Campaigners high-lighted the impact on families, but reform was slow.

Youth, Drugs, and Moral Panic

Beyond the Bulger case, youth crime dominated head-lines. Joyriding, knife crime, and gang fights were portrayed as epidemics, often disproportionately blaming working-class or minority youth. The Criminal Justice and Public Order Act (1994) increased police powers over gatherings, famously banning "music with repetitive beats" in a bid to curb raves. For teenagers, it felt like the state was legislating against their culture.

Drug use became another flashpoint. Heroin devastated some communities, while ecstasy became synonymous with club culture. Tabloids warned of "drug-crazed ravers," even as research showed most users combined weekend experi-mentation with relatively normal lives. Women were often portrayed in moral panics as both victims and villains: mothers neglecting children, or "ladettes" drinking and drug-taking. In reality, women's drug use remained lower than men's, but the gendered stereotypes were hard to escape.

Women and Justice

The 1990s saw growing recognition of crimes that had long been minimised or ignored. Domestic violence and marital rape were increasingly treated as serious offences, not private matters. The first national domestic violence helplines expanded, often staffed by women volunteers. Refuge networks, pioneered earlier, gained more recognition and funding, though services remained patchy.

The legal profession also saw change. More women qualified as solicitors and barristers, with figures like Helena Kennedy QC using their platforms to campaign on civil liberties, miscarriages of justice, and women's rights. Female judges, still rare, slowly increased in number, breaking centuries of male dominance in the judiciary.

Media, Crime, and Public Perception

Television played a central role in shaping how Britons understood crime. Crimewatch, hosted by Nick Ross and Jill Dando until her murder in 1999, asked the public to help solve cases, blending entertainment with justice. Tabloids splashed lurid headlines about "monsters" and "predators," often simplifying complex social problems into moral outrage.

The murder of Jill Dando itself revealed both the vulnerability of public figures and the power of rolling news. The coverage became a national obsession, reflecting how crime stories had become cultural events as much as legal cases.

Why It Mattered

The 1990s transformed Britain's relationship with crime and justice. DNA made policing more scientific, but miscarriages of justice persisted. Prisons grew more crowded, while private firms entered the justice system. Youth and drug culture fuelled moral panic, while women campaigned for recognition of domestic violence and sexual assault.

These problems were not new but in the 1990s they gained unprecedented visibility in law, media, and politics. Fear often outweighed fact, shaping laws and policies that would echo into the 2000s. For women, the justice system was both barrier and battleground: they were victims seeking recognition, lawyers and judges breaking glass ceilings, campaigners demanding reform.

The 1990s revealed Britain as a society both fascinated and frightened by crime, determined to be "tough," yet struggling to reconcile justice with fairness.

Mini Timeline – Crime and Justice

1990 – Strangeways prison riot sparks debate on conditions and reform

1993 – Murder of Stephen Lawrence; James Bulger case prompts debate on youth justice

1994 – Criminal Justice and Public Order Act expands police powers, targets raves

1995 – National DNA database established, first of its kind worldwide

1996 – Domestic violence helplines expand nationwide

1997 – First female High Court judges appointed in greater numbers

1999 – Murder of Jill Dando; rolling news coverage reveals new media-crime relationship

CONCLUSION – LEGACY OF THE
NINETIES

⤜⤝

*O*n 31 December 1999, Britain celebrated the dawn
of the millennium with fireworks over the Thames,
parties in every town square, and a collective sense that
anything was possible. The Millennium Dome glowed on the
Greenwich Peninsula, Tony Blair looked confidently toward
the future, and Cool Britannia seemed like more than a
marketing slogan. The 1990s had ended with the country
transformed, richer, more diverse, more connected, and
more confident than the recession-battered nation that had
watched Margaret Thatcher's tearful departure from
Downing Street nine years earlier.

The Dome itself, celebrated and derided in equal
measure, became the perfect metaphor for the decade. Bold,
noisy, ambitious, and expensive, it captured the optimism of
a country that wanted to present itself as modern and global,
while also symbolising the gap between hype and reality that
ran through much of the 1990s. For families who visited, it
was a memory of hope and spectacle; for critics, it was a
white elephant. Either way, it crystallised the contradictions
of the era.

But as the hangovers cleared and the new century began, it became apparent that the 1990s had created as many questions as answers. The decade that promised to modernise Britain had indeed done so, but modernity came with complications that nobody had fully anticipated.

THE ECONOMIC LEGACY: **Prosperity and Precarity**

The economic transformation of the 1990s established patterns that still define British life today. The shift from manufacturing to services, the dominance of financial markets, the flexible labour market, and the growing regional inequalities between London and everywhere else all became entrenched during the decade.

Gordon Brown's reforms, Bank of England independence, the golden rule, tax credits, and the minimum wage, created the macroeconomic stability that underpinned New Labour's early success. But they also embedded an economic model dependent on consumer spending, property prices, and financial services that would prove fragile in later crises.

For women, the decade brought unprecedented workforce participation and new legal protections through European Union directives. The minimum wage particularly benefited female workers in low-paid sectors. Yet the gender pay gap persisted at around 17%, and the rise of part-time, flexible work often meant exchanging security for supposed freedom. The 1990s taught women that they could have careers, but not necessarily on equal terms.

The retail revolution, Sunday shopping, out-of-town centres, coffee culture, created millions of jobs but also transformed British high streets forever. The Trafford Centre and Starbucks became symbols of a new consumer society where shopping wasn't just about necessity but identity. This culture of consumption would define the 2000s, fuel the credit boom, and ultimately contribute to the financial crisis of 2008.

POLITICAL TRANSFORMATION: The Triumph of Image

The political lessons of the 1990s proved more durable than anyone expected. The decade established that effective media management was as important as effective policy, that perception often mattered more than reality, and that traditional ideological divides had given way to battles over competence and authenticity.

Tony Blair's victory in 1997 represented the culmination of political trends that had been building throughout the decade. The focus on spin, rapid rebuttal, and coordinated messaging became the standard for all subsequent governments. Alastair Campbell's innovations in media management created a template that David Cameron, Theresa May, Boris Johnson, and their successors would all follow, with varying degrees of success.

The Conservative Party's divisions over Europe, which paralysed John Major's government and contributed to their crushing defeat, previewed the schisms that would eventually tear the party apart over Brexit. The Euroscepticism that emerged from Black Wednesday's humiliation and Maastricht's ratification battles provided the ideological foundation for the Leave campaign two decades later.

Perhaps most significantly, the 1990s established the idea that politics was a performance to be consumed rather than a civic duty to be engaged with. The transformation of politicians into celebrities, the reduction of complex issues to soundbites, and the blurring of boundaries between news and entertainment all accelerated during the decade. These changes democratised political communication but also made it more superficial and manipulative.

. . .

CULTURAL CONFIDENCE and Cultural Wars

The cultural legacy of the 1990s remains visible on every British high street. The decade's music, fashion, and art established Britain as a global cultural exporter on a scale not seen since the 1960s. Britpop bands like Oasis and Blur created anthems that still soundtrack political campaigns and sporting events. The Young British Artists, Damien Hirst, Tracey Emin, and others, redefined what contemporary art could be and do.

But the decade also institutionalised cultural battles that continue today. The tension between lad culture and Girl Power reflected deeper anxieties about changing gender roles that persist in contemporary debates about feminism, masculinity, and workplace equality. The art world controversies that made Tracey Emin's bed front-page news established a template for culture war conflicts that play out across social media platforms today.

The Spice Girls' "Girl Power" was both revolutionary and limiting, it gave a generation of girls permission to be loud, ambitious, and unapologetic, while reducing complex feminist politics to consumer choices and individual empowerment. This tension between genuine progress and commercial co-optation characterises much contemporary feminism.

The decade's celebration of British multiculturalism, chicken tikka masala as the national dish, Asian Underground music, Black British achievement in sport and culture, coexisted with the exposure of institutional racism through Stephen Lawrence's murder. This contradiction established a pattern where Britain simultaneously celebrated diversity and struggled with discrimination that remains unresolved.

. . .

Technology's **Double Edge**

The digital revolution that began in the 1990s created the infrastructure of contemporary life. The internet, mobile phones, personal computers, and satellite television all became mainstream during the decade, laying the foundation for social media, smartphones, and streaming services that now dominate daily experience.

But the decade's technological optimism proved naïve about the social consequences of digital transformation. The internet was supposed to democratise information and empower individuals, and it did, while also creating new forms of harassment, misinformation, and social division. Mobile phones promised to liberate people from fixed locations, and they did, while also creating expectations of constant availability that blurred work-life boundaries.

For women, technology offered new opportunities for connection, entrepreneurship, and expression while also creating new platforms for abuse and objectification. The patterns established in the 1990s chatrooms and early online communities previewed the harassment campaigns and gender-based violence that would proliferate across social media platforms.

The economic disruption caused by technological change, the decline of traditional media, the transformation of retail, and the casualisation of work created winners and losers in ways that politicians were slow to recognise or address. The 1990s enthusiasm for creative destruction and flexible markets looked less appealing when applied to entire industries and communities.

Social Change **and Its Limits**

The social transformations of the 1990s were real but incomplete. Women's representation in Parliament doubled overnight in 1997, but the glass ceiling in boardrooms and senior positions remained largely intact. LGBTQ+ visibility increased dramatically, but Section 28 reminded sexual minorities that tolerance had legal limits. Multiculturalism flourished in cities while racism persisted in institutions and communities.

The decade's approach to social change, celebrating diversity while avoiding structural reform, established patterns that still constrain British politics. The focus on representation and visibility, while important, often substituted for deeper changes in power and resources. The 1990s taught Britain to talk about equality while accepting inequality.

Family structures changed fundamentally during the decade, with rising divorce rates, single parenthood, and dual-income households becoming normal rather than exceptional. But childcare provision, parental leave policies, and workplace flexibility lagged behind these demographic changes. Women gained the right to work but not always the support systems to make that work sustainable.

The expansion of higher education; university participation rates rose from 19% in 1990 to 33% by 1999, democratised access to knowledge and opportunity while creating new forms of inequality based on educational credentials and student debt. The 1990s promised that education would be the great equaliser but discovered that it could also entrench advantage.

The Global and the Local

The 1990s globalization, cheap flights, international media, multicultural cuisine, expanded horizons while creating new anxieties about identity and belonging. The decade taught Britons that they were part of a global culture while making them more uncertain about what made them distinctively British.

The European question that tormented John Major's government and energised Tony Blair's opposition revealed fundamental uncertainties about Britain's place in the world. Was the country European, Atlantic, or global? Could it be all three simultaneously? The 1990s amplified these questions without resolving them, setting the stage for the Brexit conflicts that would dominate the 2010s.

The humanitarian interventions in the Balkans, the peace process in Northern Ireland, and Princess Diana's landmine campaigning showed Britain playing a positive global role as a moral superpower. But they also established expectations about international leadership that would prove impossible to sustain as other powers rose and British influence waned.

THE DIGITAL DIVIDE

Perhaps the 1990s' most lasting legacy was the establishment of digital technology as the primary driver of economic and social change. The decade's pioneers; from Tim Berners-Lee inventing the World Wide Web to Martha Lane Fox co-founding Lastminute.com, created the template for the tech entrepreneurship that would dominate the following decades.

But the benefits of digitalisation were unevenly distributed from the start. The 1990s created a digital divide between those who could afford computers and internet access and those who could not, between digital natives and digital immigrants, between tech-savvy metropolitan elites and left-behind communities still dealing with deindustrialisation.

This divide had particular implications for women, who were often excluded from the male-dominated tech industry despite being early adopters of digital communication technologies. The pattern established in the 1990s, women as users but not creators of technology, persisted into the social media age and beyond.

THE UNFINISHED REVOLUTION

The 1990s were revolutionary but incomplete. The decade dismantled many traditional structures - such as deference to authority, fixed social roles and economic certainties, without fully replacing them with new institutions and norms. The result was a society that was freer but also more insecure, more diverse but also more divided, more connected but also more fragmented.

The women's revolution exemplified this incompleteness. Women gained unprecedented access to political power, economic opportunity, and cultural visibility during the decade. But they did so within systems that remained fundamentally structured around male experiences and priorities. The result was progress that felt simultaneously dramatic and insufficient.

The 1990s established that change was possible, that ordinary people could challenge powerful institutions and win. The campaigns that secured gun control after Dunblane, peace in Northern Ireland, and justice for Stephen Lawrence showed that citizen activism could achieve extraordinary results. But they also revealed how much sustained effort was required to translate individual victories into systemic transformation.

Echoes in the Present

Walk through any British city today and the 1990s legacy is everywhere. The coffee shops and retail parks, the mobile phone stores and internet cafés (now repurposed for other uses), the multicultural restaurants and converted warehouses, the physical infrastructure of contemporary Britain was largely built during the decade.

More subtly, the cultural and political frameworks established in the 1990s continue to shape how Britain understands itself. The techniques of political communication pioneered by New Labour are now standard practice. The celebrity culture launched by Heat magazine defines contemporary media consumption. The consumer culture that replaced traditional industries as the engine of economic growth remains central to British prosperity.

The social changes initiated in the 1990s, women's workforce participation, family diversity, cultural multiculturalism, have continued to evolve, but within frameworks established during the decade. Contemporary debates about work-life balance, immigration and integration, and gender equality all use vocabulary and concepts that emerged from 1990s conflicts.

THE PROMISE and the Peril

The 1990s ended with the promise that Britain could be both prosperous and progressive, both modern and rooted, both global and local. Tony Blair's confidence that the country could master the forces of change while preserving its essential character captured the decade's optimism perfectly.

That promise proved harder to fulfil than anyone expected. The dot-com crash of 2001, the 9/11 attacks, the Iraq War, the 2008 financial crisis, and the Brexit referendum all tested the assumptions and institutions created during the 1990s. Many proved more fragile than they had appeared at the millennium's optimistic dawn.

But the decade's core insight, that Britain could reinvent itself without losing its identity, remains valid and necessary. The 1990s showed that change was possible, that ordinary people could shape extraordinary events, and that the country's best traditions of tolerance, pragmatism, and civic engagement could survive and thrive in new circumstances.

The women who doubled Parliamentary representation in 1997, who campaigned for peace in Northern Ireland, who built businesses and movements and art that changed the world, proved that progress was possible when enough people demanded it. Their legacy is not just the specific victories they achieved but the demonstration that determined activism could overcome seemingly immovable obstacles.

The Continuing Story

The 1990s didn't solve Britain's problems, they revealed them and provided some tools for addressing them. The decade's greatest gift was not its achievements but its demonstration that achievement was possible. The frameworks created for understanding diversity, technology, globalisation, and social change remain relevant even as the specific challenges have evolved.

The story that began in the 1990s of a country grappling with who it wanted to be in a changing world continues today. The questions raised by the decade about identity and belonging, prosperity and inequality, democracy and media, remain central to British politics and society.

Perhaps that's the most fitting legacy of the 1990s: they established that these questions were worth asking and that ordinary people, especially those whose voices had been excluded from traditional power structures, had essential contributions to make in answering them.

The decade that began with Margaret Thatcher's fall and ended with Tony Blair's triumph was ultimately about more than the politicians who dominated the headlines. It was about a society learning to live with diversity, to adapt to technological change, to balance global integration with local identity, and to expand opportunities while maintaining communities.

The 1990s were messy, contradictory, and often frustrating. They promised more than they delivered and solved fewer problems than they created. But they also demonstrated something essential about British society: its capacity for reinvention, its resilience in the face of change, and its gradual, grudging, but genuine progress toward becoming a more open, inclusive, and dynamic country.

That spirit of possibility, tempered by experience but not defeated by setbacks, remains the decade's most valuable legacy. The 1990s ended with the promise of a new millennium. That promise was naive, but it wasn't false. The future remained unwritten, and ordinary people, especially those who had been written out of previous stories, still had the power to shape it.

The nineties made us modern. Whether we make that modernity work for everyone remains the unfinished business of British democracy.

TIMELINE-LEGACIES OF THE NINETIES

*T*imeline – **The 90s Echo in the 2020s**
Politics & Power

1990 → 2019 – Thatcher's fall over Europe sets the stage for the Brexit divisions that would later topple Theresa May.

1992 → 2016 – Black Wednesday fuels Euroscepticism, which becomes the foundation of the Leave campaign.

1997 → 2020s – Blair's spin culture evolves into permanent media warfare on Twitter and TikTok.

1998 → 2023 – The Good Friday Agreement still underpins peace, even as Brexit tests its foundations.

1999 → 2022 – House of Lords reform unfinished; debates on a fully elected chamber continue.

Economy & Work

1991 → 2020s – Recession and negative equity echo in the housing affordability crisis of today.

1994 → 2020s – National Lottery funding still underpins grassroots sport, the arts, and heritage.

1996 → 2020s – BSE and "Frankenstein food" panics foreshadow current debates on food safety and lab-grown meat.

1999 → 2020s – The gig economy grows out of the "flexible" jobs model first normalised in the 90s.

1999 → 2023 – Y2K panic echoes in fears about AI and cybersecurity — society again worries whether machines are out of control.

Culture & Identity

1993 → 2020s – Stephen Lawrence campaign leads to continuing debates about institutional racism, now reframed by Black Lives Matter.

1994 → 2020s – Section 28 protests laid the groundwork for today's LGBTQ+ rights victories, including equal marriage.

1996 → 2022 – Girl Power anticipates later feminist movements (#MeToo, body positivity), though commercialisation debates persist.

1996 → 2020s – Lad culture resurfaces in online "banter" culture; ladette energy survives in unapologetic female voices in media.

1997 → 2020s – Harry Potter launches fantasy publishing dominance, while Rowling's later controversies spark debates about authorship, identity, and fandom.

1997 → 2020s – Teletubbies → Peppa Pig: British children's TV remains a global export.

Technology & Science

1991 → 2020s – First websites foreshadow today's dependence on the internet for everything from shopping to democracy.

1992 → 2020s – First text message becomes the DNA of WhatsApp, Instagram DMs, and TikTok comments.

1995 → 2020s – Windows 95 "start" button to today's touchscreen smartphones — personal computing goes mainstream.

1996 → 2020s – Dolly the Sheep → stem cell research, cloning ethics, and today's debates about AI-driven biology.

1997 → 2020s – DVDs → streaming wars (Netflix, Disney+).

1998 → 2020s – Google founded; still dominates how we access knowledge today.

1999 → 2020s – Napster's file-sharing revolution → Spotify, Apple Music, and streaming royalties controversies.

1990s → 2020s – Human Genome Project → personalised medicine, CRISPR gene editing.

Sport & National Pride

1990 → 2022 – Italia '90 tears → Lionesses' Euro 2022 triumph; emotional football moments unite the nation.

1992 → 2020s – Premier League launch → the richest football league in the world, watched on every continent.

1994 → 2020s – England women's rugby victory foreshadows today's professional Red Roses dominance.

1999 → 2022 – Manchester United's Treble → Premier League globalisation and superclub culture.

1990s → 2020s – Women's sport ignored then, primetime now: from back-page cricket reports to sold-out Wembley finals.

Media & Everyday Life

1993 → 2020s – "Cash for questions" sleaze → continuing debates on lobbying and political corruption.

1994 → 2020s – Friends shapes café culture → still binge-watched on Netflix today.

1995 → 2020s – Diana's Panorama interview → Harry & Meghan's Oprah interview; royals and media still entwined.

1997 → 2020s – Heat magazine, lad mags → Instagram, reality TV, Love Island gossip.

1999 → 2020s – Big Brother template → social media influencer culture.

1990s → 2020s – Millennium Dome → O2 Arena: from mocked white elephant to beloved cultural venue.

BIBLIOGRAPHY

Politics & Society

- Bogdanor, Vernon. *The New British Constitution*. Oxford: Hart Publishing, 2009.
- Evans, Eric J. *Thatcher and Thatcherism*. 3rd ed. London: Routledge, 2013.
- Kavanagh, Dennis, and David Butler. *The British General Election of 1997*. Basingstoke: Macmillan, 1997.
- Seldon, Anthony. *Blair*. London: Free Press, 2004.
- Young, Hugo. *This Blessed Plot: Britain and Europe from Churchill to Blair*. London: Macmillan, 1998.

Culture & Media

- Bracewell, Michael. *England Is Mine: Pop Life in Albion from Wilde to Goldie*. London: HarperCollins, 1997.
- Harris, John. *The Last Party: Britpop, Blair and the Demise of English Rock*. London: Harper Perennial, 2004.
- Hebdige, Dick. *Subculture: The Meaning of Style*. London: Routledge, 1979 (reprint 2002). [Influential framework for 90s cultural analysis].
- Sandbrook, Dominic. *White Heat: A History of Britain in the Swinging Sixties*. London: Abacus, 2006. [Contextual background for understanding 90s cultural developments].
- Turner, Alwyn W. *Rejoice! Rejoice! Britain in the 1980s*. London: Aurum Press, 2013.
- ——. *A Classless Society: Britain in the 1990s*. London: Aurum Press, 2013.

Sport & National Identity

- Collins, Tony. *Sport in a Capitalist Society: A Short History*. London: Routledge, 2013.
- Hughson, John, Kevin Dixon, and David Inglis. *The Uses of Sport: A Critical Study*. London: Routledge, 2005.

- Porter, Dilwyn, and Adrian Smith, eds. *Sport and National Identity in the Post-War World*. London: Routledge, 2004.
- Williams, Jean. *A Game for Rough Girls? A History of Women's Football in Britain*. London: Routledge, 2003.

Technology & Economy

- Castells, Manuel. *The Rise of the Network Society*. Oxford: Blackwell, 1996.
- Hutton, Will. *The State We're In*. London: Jonathan Cape, 1995.
- Lane Fox, Martha, and Brent Hoberman. *lastminute.com: Adventures in the Dotcom*. London: Random House, 2001.
- Singh, Simon. *The Code Book: The Secret History of Codes and Code-Breaking*. London: Fourth Estate, 1999.

Society, Identity & Change

- Hall, Stuart, and Martin Jacques, eds. *New Times: The Changing Face of Politics in the 1990s*. London: Lawrence & Wishart, 1990. [Analysis of late 1980s political transformation influencing 1990s discourse].
- Macpherson, William. *The Stephen Lawrence Inquiry*. London: The Stationery Office, 1999.
- McRobbie, Angela. *Feminism and Youth Culture: From Jackie to Just Seventeen*. London: Macmillan, 1991.
- Weeks, Jeffrey. *Coming Out: Homosexual Politics in Britain from the Nineteenth Century to the Present*. 3rd ed. London: Quartet, 1990.

www.ingramcontent.com/pod-product-compliance
Lightning Source LLC
Chambersburg PA
CBHW031128020426
42333CB00012B/276